Lernkrimi Englisch

Das Rätsel der Mumie

Story: Marc Hillefeld
Übersetzung: Karen Vaughan

Compact Verlag

Bisher sind in dieser Reihe erschienen:

- Compact Lernkrimi Englisch Grammatik
- Compact Lernkrimi Englisch Konversation
- Compact Lernkrimi Englisch Grundwortschatz
- Compact Lernkrimi Englisch Aufbauwortschatz
- Compact Lernkrimi Französisch Grundwortschatz
- Compact Lernkrimi Italienisch Grundwortschatz
- Compact Lernkrimi Spanisch Grundwortschatz
- Compact Lernkrimi Spanisch Grammatik

Weitere Titel sind in Vorbereitung.

Chefredaktion: Evelyn Boos
Redaktion: Brigitte Stoffel
Fachredaktion: Anthony Moore
Produktion: Wolfram Friedrich
Titelillustration: Karl Knospe
Typografischer Entwurf: Maria Seidel
Umschlaggestaltung: Carsten Abelbeck

ISBN 3-8174-7304-4
7273045

Besuchen Sie uns im Internet: www.compactverlag.de

Vorwort

Mit dem neuen, spannenden Compact Lernkrimi können Sie Ihre Englischkenntnisse auf schnelle und einfache Weise vertiefen, auffrischen und überprüfen.
Inspector Hudson erleichtert das Sprachtraining mit Action und Humor. Er und seine mysteriösen Kriminalfälle stehen im Mittelpunkt einer zusammenhängenden Story.
Der Krimi wird auf jeder Seite durch abwechslungsreiche und kurzweilige Übungen ergänzt, die das Lernen unterhaltsam und spannend machen.
Prüfen Sie Ihr Englisch in Lückentexten, Zuordnungs- und Übersetzungsaufgaben, in Buchstabenspielen und Kreuzworträtseln!
Ob im Bus oder in der Bahn, im Wartezimmer, zu Hause oder in der Mittagspause – das Sprachtraining im handlichen Format bietet die ideale Trainingsmöglichkeit für zwischendurch.
Schreiben Sie die Lösungen einfach ins Buch!
Die richtigen Antworten sind in einem eigenen Lösungsteil zusammengefasst.

Und nun kann die Spannung beginnen …

Viel Spaß und Erfolg!

Inhalt

Story

James Hudson arbeitet als Inspector bei der legendären Polizeibehörde Scotland Yard. Er ist einer der fähigsten Männer und wird immer dann zu Rate gezogen, wenn seine Kollegen mal wieder vor einem Rätsel stehen. Seine resolute und krimibegeisterte Haushälterin Miss Paddington unterstützt ihn stets mit liebevoller Fürsorge. Und insgeheim verfolgt sie noch ein weiteres Ziel: ihn endlich mit der jungen, attraktiven Versicherungsagentin Elvira Elliot zu verkuppeln.

Im Londoner British Museum wurde auf unerklärliche Weise eine wertvolle Mumie gestohlen!
Inspector Hudson geht auf die Suche nach dem Täter und gerät in einen Kriminalfall, der zunehmend mysteriöser wird …
Wer könnte ein Motiv haben, eine fünftausend Jahre alte Mumie zu stehlen? Ist der Fluch des Pharao nur ein Aberglaube? Wird dieser geheimnisvolle Fall noch ein weiteres Menschenleben fordern?
Nach und nach gelingt es Inspector Hudson, Licht in das Dunkel des Unerklärlichen zu bringen …

The Mystery of the Mummy

Inspector James Hudson loved the soft noises that penetrated his flat on Baker Street early in the morning. Especially when he had a day off work, which rarely happened. How often had his housekeeper, Miss Paddington, insisted that he use up some of his overtime and stay at home in the morning. Usually at this time, he would have already been in his small office at Scotland Yard for quite a while, answering urgent phone-calls, interrogating witnesses or examining crime sites. However, today was different.

Übung 1: Unterstreichen Sie die regelmäßigen Verben im Simple Past!

James sighed deeply and closed his eyes, while he let himself sink down in his armchair. He could feel the calmness rubbing off on him. Still, he could not simply turn off his detective instincts. Breathing slowly and calmly, he listened to the tranquillity and tried to identify the noises which could be heard every so often. This was a relaxation exercise for him and at the same time concentration training.

To begin with, there was the old grandfather clock in the corner of the living room. Its steady ticking was like a heartbeat in the stillness. Or perhaps like a calming rhythm giving order to all the noises.

Suddenly James jumped, without opening his eyes. While the clock's ticking was a steady rhythm, from the kitchen came a crashing sound followed by Miss Paddington's curses. His housekeeper had probably dropped a pot or something. The inspector grinned at the old lady's curses, which were anything but ladylike, and continued his concentration exercise. Until this moment it had been quite simple.

A patter on the windowpane suggested it had begun to rain. Nothing unusual in London at this time of the year.

Or at any other time of the year …

! ÜBUNG 2

Übung 2: Setzen Sie die Verben ins Simple Past!

Mr Hudson (1. to smile) ______________ to himself as he (2. to wait) ______________ for the next noise. The clock struck eight.

Aaand … there it was. A muffled thump on the door.

Mr Hudson's smile widened.

Every time it (3. to rain) ________________, the paperboy, Tim, (4. not to do) ___________________ bother to put the London Times in the post box. He simply threw it in front of the house door, where this respectable printed newspaper soaked up the rain, if Miss Paddington did not quickly bring it in.

James Hudson could already hear his housekeeper as she (5. to grumble) ______________ when she (6. to go) ______________ to open the door cursing the paperboy. However, the squeaking of a rusty bicycle chain told him that Tim (7. to be) ______________ already well on his way and probably ignoring the elderly lady completely.

Mr Hudson still (8. to think) ________ everything was proceeding as usual, when he was puzzled by yet another noise: despite the pattering rain, it took Miss Paddington a few seconds to close the door behind her. That could only mean one thing. She must have been startled by the headlines on the first page of the Times. James (9. to frown) ____________________. Miss Paddington had been his housekeeper for many years now. He knew the determined old lady was not easily shaken. And that meant only one thing. Hudson sighed again, opened his eyes and waited.

A minute later Miss Paddington (10. to enter) _________________ the living room. She was holding a silver tray on which there were a steaming teapot of tea, a couple of slices of bread, some marmalade – and the slightly wet morning edition of the London Times.

"Good morning, Mr Hudson," she said with slight disapproval in her voice. "On your day off, you could have slept in, you know?"

James (11. to laugh) ____________________. "It's not that easy to change one's habits, my dear Miss Paddington."

"You work too hard," (12. to answer) _____________ Miss Paddington in a slightly disapproving tone of voice.

"Well, crime does not sleep either, Miss Paddington," (13. to reply) ________________ James and pointed at the newspaper.

"So, what new crime is about to spoil my day off work – apart from the weather?"
Miss Paddington gasped in surprise and placed the tray on the small coffee table near the armchair.

ÜBUNG 3 !

Übung 3: Welches Wort ist das „schwarze Schaf"?

1. my, your, his, walk, her ______
2. in, by, from, yesterday, for ______
3. enter, house, do, dream, dance ______
4. crime, theft, robbery, search ______
5. wet, hot, book, rainy ______
6. he, they, it, man ______
7. happily, awfully, dry, well ______
8. silence, tranquillity, calm, noise ______

"H-How did you know that again, James?"
Miss Paddington always tended to call her young employer by his first name, when she was surprised. And this was obviously the case. James poured himself a cup of tea and smiled. "I heard you wait a second longer before bringing in the newspaper. And I deduced that you were alarmed by the headlines. And since you are not easy to alarm, that can only mean two things: either the Queen of England has run away with a stableman –"
"Heaven forbid!" exclaimed Miss Paddington. "That is not a thing to joke about!"

"– or," continued Mr Hudson, "an unusual crime has been committed, which must be in my field of activity."

Miss Paddington shook her head in admiration. "Thank God for the latter, sir." Miss Paddington, an enthusiastic reader of crime novels and a hobby detective herself, was fascinated each time by the inspector's powers of deduction. Sometimes James believed that his housekeeper had adopted him on the spot only to have a real criminal investigator in the family.

"Let's see," said James as he picked up the newspaper from the tray. What he read on the first page was indeed unusual. So unusual he had to read the short sentence twice, to make sure he had not misunderstood it.

'SHOCKING MUMMY THEFT AT BRITISH MUSEUM' glared the headlines on the wet newspaper's first page.

"Who on earth would steal a mummy," asked Miss Paddington shaking her head.

Übung 4: Beantworten Sie die folgenden Fragen zum Text im Präsens!

ÜBUNG 4 !

1. Where does Mr Hudson live?

____

2. Who is Miss Paddington?

____

3. What noises can Mr Hudson hear?

____

4. What does Mr Hudson have for breakfast?

---

5. Which newspaper does Mr Hudson read?

"I have no idea," replied Hudson, "but I'm afraid it will be my job to find that out." He glanced at the old grandfather clock. It was 8.14. He took a quick gulp of his tea, stood up and went to the phone in the corridor and waited.

ÜBUNG 5 !

Übung 5: Unterstreichen Sie die unregelmäßigen Verben im Simple Past und überlegen Sie sich die Stammform!

Hudson did not have to wait for long. After two or three minutes the old-fashioned phone rang. Miss Paddington let out a loud, very audible sigh. She had a feeling that the inspector's day off was over. James let the phone ring twice – he thought it was impolite to pick up the receiver after the first ring – before answering.
"Good morning, Sir Reginald," said Hudson politely. The inspector knew that only one person could be on the other end of the line.

His superior at the Scotland Yard, Sir Reginald.
Although James Hudson was only an ordinary inspector at Scotland Yard, his advice was always needed for mysterious and unusual crimes. Normal cases such as bank robberies, or a basic crime of violence had not been in his field of activity for years. Every time anything bizarre happened, the case was assigned to him.
And without any doubt the case of the missing mummy would end up on Hudson's desk.

If this theft had made it to the first page of the Times, then with all probability there was already a crowd of reporters in his senior's office.

"Hudson!" barked Sir Reginald down the receiver. "I need you here!" Sir Reginald did not bother to return Hudson's greeting. If James was a tracker dog, then Sir Reginald was a bulldog! Tranquil and friendly when left alone, but snappish when someone treads on his toes.

Hudson smiled slightly as he remembered that Sir Reginald even looked a little like a bulldog.

Übung 6: Übersetzen Sie und enträtseln Sie das Lösungswort!

1. Hinweis ☐ _ _ _
2. Raub _ _ _ _ _ ☐ _
3. herausfinden _ ☐ _ _   _ _ _
4. Mord ☐ _ _ _ _ _
5. Polizei _ _ _ _ _ ☐

Lösung: _ _ _ _ _

"Hudson, I have a pack of journalists on my back who want to know something about the case of the missing mummy. I only read about it this morning in the newspaper. Good heavens, who would be stupid enough to steal a mummy?!"

"No idea, sir," replied Hudson smiling. "But I have a feeling you want me to find that out."

"Anyhow!" barked Sir Reginald. "Go to the museum at once, so that I can at least tell these nosy-parkers and stupid reporters that

I've put my best man on this difficult and mysterious job."
"Very flattering, sir," said Hudson, "but may I just remind you that today's my day off?"
"Never mind. We'll talk about that later." Having said that, Sir Reginald abruptly rang off.
Hudson smiled. Any other reaction would have surprised him. To be honest with himself, he was actually very pleased about the new unexpected assignment. A day off with nothing to do could be nerve-racking. And the case of the missing mummy sounded interesting indeed. Sir Reginald had a point: what idiot would steal a mummy thousands of years old and, above all, why?
Well, he would find that out.

ÜBUNG 7 !

Übung 7: Setzen Sie den richtigen Artikel ein!
*(**a**, **an**, **the** oder nichts)*

1. Last night ____________ mummy was stolen from ________ British Museum.
2. Mr Hudson lives in ___________ big flat downtown.
3. ___________ elderly couple was crossing the road when ___________ police car drove by.
4. How much is the ticket for the museum? Fifteen pounds ___________ day.
5. How often does Miss Paddignton watch the news? Once ___________ hour.
6. ___________ fear is horrible.

7. I read ____________ headlines ____________ minute ago.

8. ____________ English love drinking tea.

Whistling happily, he walked into the kitchen where Miss Paddington was busy again with her pots and pans. She observed the inspector's smile suspiciously.
"My dear Miss Paddington," said Hudson and prepared himself for trouble, "I'm afraid my day off work has come to an end. Sir Reginald needs me."
Miss Paddington banged a pan on the stove. "My dear Mr Hudson," she said reprovingly, "you specifically promised me that you would rest today. After the case of the Tower Bridge ghost you certainly have earned the right to a break."
Hudson shuddered at the thought of that crime. He had closed the case only a week before – and he had almost lost his life.
"Nothing comforts me more, Miss Paddington, than a little mystery which needs to be solved. And besides, nothing much can happen to anyone looking for a five-thousand-year old mummy," chuckled the inspector.
But how wrong he was indeed!

Übung 8: Wie lautet der Plural dieser Wörter?

ÜBUNG 8 !

1. newspaper ____________

2. thief ____________

3. woman ____________

4. man ____________

5. potato ______________

6. mouse ______________

7. knife ______________

8. ox ______________

9. fox ______________

10. lobby ______________

A few minutes later, Mr Hudson was dressed according to the weather. He said goodbye to Miss Paddington and got into his car. The Bentley's engine spluttered protestingly as he turned the ignition key. Such an old car felt the weather just like any human would.

At last, after three more attempts the engine started. Rattling loudly the heavy car jerked forward through the rainy streets.

Hudson had been driving the car for many years and still managed to create a sensation. When passers-by on the street saw this type of precious car, they all expected a smooth moving car with a purring engine. But a Bentley, too, grows old sooner or later and shares the same destiny as any other automobile. The engine rattled, the exhaust pipe emanated strange noises and rust stains were becoming visible.

Such old Bentleys were not often seen around. Probably because people who could afford a luxury car, could also afford a new luxury car.

The inspector didn't care. He liked the comfortable seats and its steady hold on the road. He would never ever have exchanged it for a smaller Japanese car. At the most, for a new limousine, but of course he couldn't afford that with his small inspector's income.

Übung 9: Stellen Sie zu den Antworten die richtigen Fragen! Verwenden Sie folgende Wörter: ***what, where, how, whose, when, why, how much/many/often***

1. Mr Hudson lives in Baker Street.

___

2. He goes to work by car.

___

3. That's his car.

___

4. It's a Bentley.

___

5. He reads the newspaper every morning.

___

6. The museum closes at five o'clock.

___

7. She's his housekeeper.

___

8. It's about a missing mummy.

___

9. Six pounds.

___

10. He closed his last case a week before.

____

11. Because it has a comfortable seat and holds the road well.

____

Perhaps he could turn a couple of his cases into detective books and earn a lot of money. If only he didn't hate detective books so much. He was so deep in thought that he did not notice a small red sports car following him through the streets of London.
When Hudson arrived at the museum there was already a lot of excitement. The main entrance was surrounded by a large crowd of photographers and reporters.

ÜBUNG 10 !

Übung 10: Ordnen Sie die Buchstaben zu einem sinnvollen Wort!

It was useless to try and enter the museum through the main door, so the inspector drove his car around the (1. giinulbd) ______________________.

A few minutes later Hudson had found what he was looking for. An unguarded warehouse (2. rentncae) ______________. He parked his car near the entrance and got out. Cold (3. inar) ______________ hit his face, but, like all Londoners, he was accustomed to it. Undisturbed, he went inside the (4. eummus) ______________.

After going through a couple of rather uninviting storage rooms, he came to the actual display rooms.

Although time was pressing, James (5. ppedsto) ____________ for a few seconds and breathed in deeply. He loved the (6. emsll) ____________ of these ancient rooms. As a school kid he had come here on class outings to (7. idscorve) ____________ the world.

The world's most important ancient civilizations were put on display here, such as ancient Greece, the Romans or the South American Incas. And of course the Egyptians. Hudson cleared his throat and set to his task once again. A blue arrow pointed in the direction of the Egyptian area of the museum. With nearly child-like joy James Hudson ran up the steps to the first floor where some irreplaceable relics from ancient Egypt were displayed. He did not need to follow the blue arrow as he remembered his way very well.

Übung 11: Welche Synonyme gehören zusammen?
Setzen Sie die richtige Nummer in das Kästchen!

1. display	☐ rob
2. see	☐ gather evidence
3. find out	☐ do
4. make	☐ catch
5. help	☐ run away
6. investigate	☐ exhibit
7. arrest	☐ look
8. escape	☐ discover
9. steal	☐ assist

Because of the shocking theft, the museum was closed to the public. Hudson's steps echoed in the silence until he finally reached the 'Egyptian Hall'.

And here the silence was broken. The room was swarming with numerous policemen in plain clothes and in uniforms, taking photos and finger prints as well as measurements. Hudson was pleased. He loved the precision and devotion with which the policemen investigated the scene of a crime. Each little clue was carefully gathered. And in the end one had many pieces of a puzzle, which could be put together to solve the case.

"May I help you, sir?" a voiced asked behind him. It was more of a reproach than a question.

Hudson turned around and faced a grim bobby with an enormous moustache who was glaring at him.

"You certainly may, constable," said Hudson politely, "by telling me what precisely happened here."

"That has nothing to do with you, sir," answered the policeman. "This is the scene of a crime and the museum is closed to the public today."

"That's bad enough," said Hudson, "I'm sure many school classes will be standing outside in the rain very disappointed."

The constable looked confused.

! ÜBUNG 12

Übung 12: Wie heißt das Simple Past der folgenden unregelmäßigen Verben?

1. catch ________________
2. steal ________________
3. know ________________

4. shake ______________
5. bring ______________
6. see ______________
7. come ______________
8. go ______________
9. begin ______________
10. win ______________
11. sleep ______________
12. take ______________
13. can ______________
14. eat ______________
15. have ______________

"Anyway, I'm Inspector James Hudson from Scotland Yard. Sir Reginald has assigned me to this case."
The look on the constable's face became friendlier on the spot. "Oh, I'm so terribly sorry, sir. How was I to know that? I was not informed that someone from Scotland Yard was coming."
"Don't worry, old friend," replied Hudson. "I took the liberty of letting myself in."
The policeman's face had an enquiring expression.
"Oh, forget it," said Hudson quickly. He did not wish to confuse the man unnecessarily. "So where was our dead man kidnapped?"
"The mummy, I mean. Where was it stolen?" Inspector Hudson explained himself.

ÜBUNG 13 !

Übung 13: Lesen Sie weiter und unterstreichen Sie die Substantive!

"Hmm, I understand. Please follow me. I'll take you there." Hudson followed the constable across the large room. On his way to the site of the crime, Hudson looked around. The pieces exhibited had not changed much since his childhood. As the Egyptian empire had ceased to exist thousands of years ago. In the meantime there had not been many new findings. And when new relics were found, most of them stayed in Egypt where they belonged.

As a child Hudson had already wondered what the British would think if, all of a sudden, Egyptians were to make an expedition to their country to break into ancient Celtic tombs and take the treasures back with them. Here in the British Museum the treasures and relics would at least be looked after carefully.
Well, that's what he thought until the constable led him to a shattered display case. The glass box in which the mummy had been propped up was about two metres high and a metre wide. The front panel had been smashed. Inside glass splinters shone like small diamonds under the electric light from the ceiling.

ÜBUNG 14 !

Übung 14: Geben Sie die verneinte Form an!

1. I am ____________
2. We are ____________
3. He was ____________
4. I will ____________
5. I did ____________

6. She can ______________

7. He stole ______________

8. You have stolen ______________

9. I've got ______________

10. He steals ______________

11. You dream ______________

"How awful!" exclaimed Hudson.
The constable added, "Who would do anything like this?"
"That," said Hudson for the second time that day, "is what I intend to find out. Have you found any clues?"
The constable shook his head.
"The thief obviously got into the museum without breaking anything. The burglar alarm was not activated. Whoever entered the building, came here directly, broke open the display case and walked off with the mummy."

Übung 15: Setzen Sie das passende Synonym ein:
(scene, recalled, grin, brusque, enquired, criminal, surprised)

ÜBUNG 15 !

"Mmm, that means the (1. culprit) ______________ had access to the building. Perhaps even a key!"

"Maybe there isn't a culprit," said a (2. gruff) ______________ voice next to them. Hudson and the constable looked around (3. startled) ______________.

Behind them stood a sour-looking man in grey overalls. He was holding a broom in his hand. A cigar hung out of the corner of his mouth, leaving ash all around the crime (4. site) _____________. Hudson could not avoid a (5. smile) __________________. If he (6. remembered) ___________ rightly, that was the same caretaker who told them off when, as kids, they had run through the entrance or had talked too loudly.

"What do you mean by that, sir?" (7. asked) _____________ the constable. "And please be careful, the forensic check is still not finished!"

"Grrrr," grunted the caretaker and, shaking his head in the direction of the smashed glass, said, "Tut-Enk-Ra's mummy was in there. The sun king."

"Yes?" said Hudson curiously.

"Well, there are many stories about the old man, you know. When he was alive, he laid a curse on anyone who disturbed his deathbed. And, indeed, it appears that there were numerous mysterious deaths among the people who took part in the excavations."

"How interesting," said Hudson, lost in thought. "And what would your conclusion be, sir?"

The caretaker let out a thick puff of smoke. The constable coughed loudly.

"I think the mummy might have simply walked out of his display case of his own accord. You know, to take revenge on the descendants of the expeditionists, or the likes."

"You watch too many movies," interrupted the constable.

"What rubbish!"
Hudson nodded.
"I have to agree with the constable on one point."
Hudson pointed at the glass splinters inside the broken glass case.

Übung 16: Bilden Sie die fehlenden Formen!

	Infinitiv	Past	Past Participle
1.	lose	________	________
2.	________	rang	________
3.	________	________	thought
4.	wake	________	________
5.	________	spoke	________
6.	________	________	stolen
7.	shoot	________	________
8.	________	________	sat
9.	pay	________	________
10.	________	hit	________
11.	teach	________	________

"If the mummy had really walked out on his own, the glass splinters would be all around the display case. Instead they're inside. That means the glass panel was smashed in from the outside."
The caretaker shrugged his shoulders. "Perhaps the mummy had an accomplice."

"I rather think," laughed Hudson, "that Prince Tut-Enk-Ra did not leave his glass home of his own free will."
"Well, whatever," growled the caretaker, holding his broom, "I have to tidy up the whole mess."
"Don't you dare!" cried the constable. "You can't simply sweep away the clues. Take your broom away!"
The caretaker growled at the policeman. And Hudson had to come between them before it turned into a serious fight.
He laid his hand on the caretaker's shoulder.
"Tell me," he asked, "isn't there a surveillance system here?"
"Do you mean a video camera?"
"Exactly."
"Sure," replied the caretaker, "here everything is state-of-the-art. Do you think the thief was filmed while he stole the mummy?"
"That won't be difficult to find out. All we need to do is look at last night's tapes. Please take me to the security guards' room."
"Certainly," grunted the caretaker.
Hudson followed the grumbling old man and, turning towards the constable, said "And leave everything in order when you have finished here, OK, constable?"
The policeman nearly saluted him. "Yes, sir inspector!"

! ÜBUNG 17

Übung 17: Sind die folgenden Sätze inhaltlich richtig oder falsch? Markieren Sie: richtig ✔ falsch –

1. The policeman and the caretaker had a fist fight.
2. The mummy was lying in his display case.
3. State-of-the-art means the current stage of development of a practical or technological subject.
4. The alarm was activated when the thief entered the museum.

5. Some of the people who dug up Tut-Enk-Ra's grave died.
6. The mummy's display case was made of iron.
7. The caretaker swept away the clues with his broom.

Ten minutes later, Inspector Hudson was sitting in a room with very futuristic equipment. On the one wall over a dozen monitors were flickering and surveying all the museum's rooms. As the British Museum was still closed, the Egyptian area was the only place where any activity was going on. Hudson could see that the policemen were slowly packing away their instruments and cameras. The forensic test was nearly over.
"Could we watch all the tapes videoed last night?" Mr Hudson asked the man at the control desk.
"Of course ..." said the technician and pressed a few buttons.
He seemed rather excited at the idea of helping Scotland Yard in an investigation. His job was probably normally dead boring.
Hudson concentrated on the monitor in front of him. The Egyptian hall could clearly be seen, filmed by a camera on the white ceiling.

*Übung 18 : Setzen Sie **a/an** oder **some** ein!*

ÜBUNG 18 !

1. ________ alibi 2. ________ tree 3. ________ money 4. ________ tomato 5. ________ job 6. ________ music 7. ________ apple 8. ________ work 9. ________ investigation 10. ________ evidence 11. ________ information

The camera moved around the room and also videoed the display case with the mummy. The shrouded corpse of Tut-Enk-Ra stood

unmoving, just as it had been doing so for thousands of years.
"Shall I wind the tape forward?" asked the technician.
Hudson did not really feel like watching the nightly happenings of the museum hall in real time.
"Yes, if possible," he said.
"No problem."
The technician pressed another couple of buttons and the recording started to move wildly across the screen.
"I can wind it forward even faster, if you wish, sir," said the technician.
"That'll do," replied Hudson.
He was already getting dizzy.
He concentrated carefully on the screen. The camera moved from left to right and back again at the speed of lightning.
Again and again.
Nothing.

ÜBUNG 19 !

Übung 19: Welche Gegenteile gehören zusammen?
Schreiben Sie die Nummer in das richtige Kästchen!

1. reply	☐ dry
2. rainy	☐ start
3. speak	☐ happy
4. yes	☐ hot
5. finish	☐ healthy
6. sad	☐ calm
7. cold	☐ listen
8. panic	☐ ask
9. sick	☐ no

Suddenly Hudson thought he saw something like a shadow flash across the picture.
"Stop the tape!" he ordered.
The technician had also noticed it, because at that exact moment he pressed the 'pause' button.
The picture froze.
Both men bent forward and were hypnotized by the screen.
No doubt about it, the silhouette of a man moved towards the mummy's glass case. He was holding a long object in his hand.
An iron bar.
"Please play the tape at a normal speed."
The technician pressed a button. The frozen picture started moving again. The man took a few steps towards the glass case. He was wearing some black overalls and his whole face, except for his eyes, was covered by a cloth.

Übung 20: Lesen Sie weiter und setzen Sie die richtigen Präpositionen in die Lücken ein!

Whoever it was, he knew he was being watched 1. _______ a camera. Hudson also noticed something else. At first he thought it was some kind of a disturbance 2. _______ the screen, but, looking 3. _______ it for the second time, he was absolutely sure: the man limped. He dragged his left leg only very slightly, but once detected, the limp could not be ignored.

Hudson made a mental note. The limp was not a breakthrough, but perhaps a first and important clue which helps to find the mean thief. On the monitor the man had now reached the showcase. He lifted the iron bar and without hesitating smashed the glass. On the mute videotape, the breaking glass could not be heard. Hudson and the technician watched as the man carefully took the mummy out 4. _______ the glass box and carried it away. The camera moved again and once it had focussed 5. _______ the showcase again, both the man and the mummy had disappeared.

"Well we've just caught the thief red-handed on film and still haven't made any progress," said Hudson 6. _______ a sigh.

"Please send the tape to Scotland Yard," he told the technician. "The guys 7. _______ the technical department might be able to find out something else about the thief."

Puzzled, Hudson stood up and went to the door.

"Oh, by the way," he said, "is there any such thing as a list with all the people who have a key to the museum?"

"An access card," corrected the technician.

"A what?" asked Hudson.

"An electronic access card. A bit like a credit card, sir. Only this card opens the doors to the museum. Normal keys are nowhere near as safe. If you have a moment, I'd be happy to print you a list with all the names."

Hudson sighed.

It did not sound as if the list would be very short.

A quarter of an hour later, Hudson got into his Bentley. On the passenger's seat lay a sheet of paper with the names of two dozen card possessors.

Übung 21: Übersetzen Sie folgende Sätze!

ÜBUNG 21 !

1. Inspector Hudson liebte die leisen Geräusche.

2. James ließ das Telefon zweimal klingeln.

3. Er las die Titelseite nochmals.

4. Eine Minute später trat Miss Paddington ins Wohnzimmer.

5. Der Constable blickte ihn verwirrt an.

6. Vielleicht hatte die Mumie einen Komplizen.

7. Hudson konzentrierte sich auf den Bildschirm.

Things had started well.
Inspector Hudson drove his car through the centre of London.

Luckily it was late morning and the first rush hour was over. This is where, in the early morning hours, cars drove bumper to bumper. But now Hudson had a clear road.

Actually, after visiting the museum, he had intended to go to Scotland Yard. But then he had noticed the red sports car that had been following him for at least a quarter of an hour.

Of course it could have been a coincidence, but Hudson had been working for Scotland Yard too long to believe in coincidences.

ÜBUNG 22 !

*Übung 22: Setzen Sie **any** oder **some** ein!*

1. Mr Hudson hasn't collected ________ evidence on the case yet.
2. Miss Paddington bought ________ tea, but the grocer didn't have ________ bread.
3. I don't have ________ free time today. Sorry.
4. I haven't got ________ paper.
5. Would you like ________ milk?
6. Yes thank you. I would love ________.
7. I don't have ________ money in my purse.

"Let's see, my little friend," murmured Hudson, "who we are dealing with."

The inspector pressed his foot on the accelerator. The old Bentley protested – it was not accustomed to this treatment – and jerked forward.

Hudson drove elegantly through an orange traffic light – and did

not believe his eyes. Although Hudson himself had gone through the orange traffic light, the sports car's engine roared and the car, too, raced through the busy intersection.
Cars hooted and shocked drivers cursed the person of the sports car. Whoever was driving that car, Hudson thought to himself, really had good nerves.
An accident could have easily happened.
The sports car – an expensive European make that Hudson didn't know – was driven by either a madman or a reporter hoping to get a headline for some tabloid newspaper.
"If you continue driving like that," murmured Hudson to himself, "you'll end up writing your story in prison or in hospital."
The inspector spun the steering wheel around and turned suddenly into a side-street. The sports car followed him with a screeching of wheels. A couple of pedestrians jumped aside in panic.
The inspector shook his head.
Such a wild chase was fun all right, but it put innocent passers-by in danger.

Übung 23: Wie lauten die Sätze? Passen Sie auf die Adverbien auf!

! ÜBUNG 23

1. you the Do go to often museum?

____

2. because never drink I don't tea I it like

____

3. never Hudson for is work late

____

4. housekeeper watches My always evening in the news the

5. inspector has The rarely a off day

6. The suddenly car braked old

7. cars The at loudly the hooted pedestrians

He looked at the road ahead and saw the large luminous sign of a parking garage. He turned the headlights on and followed the winding way up.

The sports car was close behind and – believe it or not – even flashed its lights at Hudson.

Only a reporter could have had such a courage, or perhaps someone even worse.

Hudson drove his Bentley to the topmost floor of the parking space, steered it into a free parking place and turned the engine off.

ÜBUNG 24 !

Übung 24: Unterstreichen Sie die Adverbien!

Behind him the sportscar's engine roared. Wheels screeched and the car braked violently as it pulled into the parking space next to the Bentley.

The inspector got out.

The door of the sports car also opened. The first thing Hudson saw was a short, red mop of hair.

"Do you buy your cars to match your hair colour, Elvira?" asked the inspector.
"James, my goodness, you drive like lightning. One could get the impression that you were trying to get rid of me."
"Tut, tut," replied Hudson, "what makes you think that? Only because you have the habit of putting your nose into my investigations and putting me into tricky situations?"
Elvira Elliot was a young woman in her thirties and by trade an insurance agent for an important insurance company in London. Similarly to Hudson at the Yard, Miss Elliot was always assigned to the unsolvable cases. More than once she had prevented her company from paying costly damages, because she had recovered stolen or missing valuable goods. And she was obviously very well paid for her services, thought the inspector looking at the brand new sports car. Elvira noticed this.
"Do you like it?" she asked proudly and snobbishly at the same time.

"I bought it during my last holiday in Europe."
"Mmm," answered the inspector and had to admit to himself that he was starting to sound like the grumpy caretaker at the museum. Actually, he liked Elvira a lot – although he would never have admitted it.

*Übung 25: Setzen Sie die richtige Präposition **at**, **in** oder **on** ein!*

1. ________ six o'clock
2. ________ Saturday
3. ________ Christmas

4. ________ 1998

5. ________ the morning

6. ________ night

7. ________ midday

8. ________ dusk

9. ________ Easter Sunday

10. ________ winter

11. ________ October

12. ________ the airport

Unlike him, Elvira was a nervous person who drew conclusions too quickly and was inclined to take hasty decisions.

Although apparently with good results.

“Come on. Don’t pull such a face, James,” Elvira said laughing.

“I had a feeling you would take on the case of the stolen mummy and I’ve been following you since you left your house this morning. I’m very interested in this case, perhaps we could work together again this time.”

The inspector shook his head.

“No chance,” he said quickly. “Last time we worked together I nearly lost my job.”

Elvira bowed her head and then looked at Hudson with big eyes.

“Was it that bad? Don’t you like me at all, James. Not even a teeny weeny bit?”

“That has nothing to do with it,” replied Hudson, blushing.

“Our investigative methods are simply different.”

"And that is exactly why we complement one another so well," cried Elvira. "Come on!"
The inspector shook his head, although he was not as convinced as a minute before.
"What interest do you have in this case?" he asked. "Why are you interested in a three-thousand-year-old mummy? I thought you liked crispy young men?"
"Not only," replied Elvira looking at the inspector meaningfully. "I'm also interested in ancient Egyptian princes, when they're worth a couple of million pounds."
Hudson swallowed hard.

Übung 26: Adverb und Adjektiv bedeuten nicht dasselbe! Ordnen Sie die Übersetzungen richtig zu: ***gesund, gerade, nur, ziemlich, einzig, gut, gerecht, hübsch***

! ÜBUNG 26

1. well ______________________________

2. pretty ______________________________

3. only ______________________________

4. just ______________________________

James Hudson looked at Elvira Elliot over the edge of his tea cup. After the little hunt and the conversation in the parking garage, both had gone to a small café – Hudson had insisted on taking the Bentley – where they had been talking now for over a quarter of an hour.
Elvira waved her hand at the waiter to order her second coffee.
No wonder, the woman was always so overexcited, Hudson thought to himself as he sipped his Earl Grey tea.

Übung 27: Setzen Sie die Verben ins Present Perfect!

1. catch ______________
2. know ______________
3. shake ______________
4. bring ______________
5. see ______________
6. come ______________
7. go ______________
8. begin ______________
9. win ______________
10. sleep ______________
11. take ______________
12. can ______________

"So," he asked Elvira, once her coffee had been served, "what makes you think the mummy is worth a couple of million pounds? I mean, I know its archaeological worth is inestimable. But I don't believe the British Museum would have insured it for that much."
Elvira took a sip of coffee and smiled like a sphinx.
"Strictly speaking, it's not just about the mummy," she admitted smiling. "This old prince Tut-Enk-Rap –"
"Tut-Enk-Ra," corrected Hudson.
"– this old friend wasn't actually insured for much. Who would have dreamt that a mummy could be stolen. I really mean, a shrouded corpse is not exactly the kind of thing someone puts in

his front garden to enjoy a romantic summer evening."
Hudson nodded. The motive would be an important clue as to who the thief was; it certainly wasn't a common burglar.
"In other words," Elvira continued, "the insurance premium is hardly worth mentioning. Peanuts, so to say."
Hudson shook his head. When someone like Elvira spoke of peanuts, then it usually implied more money than he would ever earn at the Yard.

Übung 28: Unterstreichen Sie die richtige Form des Präsens!

1. Mr Hudson always works/is working overtime.
2. It rains/It's raining at the moment.
3. Hudson lives/is living in London.
4. What does Mr Hudson drink/is Mr Hudson drinking at the moment?
5. He looks/is looking for clues.
6. Miss Paddington brings/is bringing Mr Hudson breakfast every morning.
7. Hudson thinks/is thinking Elvira jumps to conclusions.

"Then why are you so interested, Elvira? Is business so bad, you are now chasing the small fish? Perhaps you shouldn't go on holiday so often and bring back little cars as souvenirs."
Elvira laughed, eyes flashing.
"Since when have you become so sarcastic, dear James. I like it."
She took another sip of coffee. Hudson noticed that the cup was already empty again.
"Don't look so surprised, James. Coffee increases your ability to concentrate and makes you happy. With this weather I need it."

ÜBUNG 29 !

Übung 29: Setzen Sie die fehlenden Wörter ein!
(meeting, tip, party, over, impatiently, drizzling, throat)

The inspector quickly looked outside. It was 1. ______________ and drops of rain were running down the window pane.

His attention was diverted for a couple of seconds, then he concentrated on Elvira again. Actually he was enjoying this cosy little 2. ______________ with the pretty insurance agent, but after all he did have a case to solve. Sir Reginald was probably waiting 3. ______________.

"So Elvira, why are you interested in the case? So much so, that you are ready to sit with me in a boring cafè, instead of enjoying yourself at one of those high-society 4. ______________ with the rich and beautiful?"

"Oh, actually I quite like sitting here with you!" replied Elvira and looked Hudson in the eyes. She burst out laughing when his ears turned red.

Then she cleared her 5. ______________ and became serious.

"Do you know, James, that the mummy theft is only the 6. ______________ of the iceberg. For the last two months ancient Egyptian objects have been disappearing all 7. ______________ England and even in Europe and the States."

The inspector became very attentive … "Disappearing?"

"Yes, they have been reported as stolen. Look here," said Elvira and glanced at Hudson with wide opened eyes.

Übung 30: Welcher Satz enthält die richtige Zeitform? Kreuzen Sie an!

ÜBUNG 30 !

1. Mr Hudson kennt Miss Paddington seit vielen Jahren.
   a) ☐ Mr Hudson knows Miss Paddington for many years.
   b) ☐ Mr Hudson has known Miss Paddington many years.
   c) ☐ Mr Hudson has known Miss Paddington for many years.

2. Ich habe viele Länder in meinem Leben besucht.
   a) ☐ I has been to many countries in my life.
   b) ☐ I have been to many countries in my life.
   c) ☐ I went to many countries in my life.

3. Was hast du gestern Abend gemacht?
   a) ☐ What do you do last night?
   b) ☐ What have you done last night?
   c) ☐ What did you do last night?

4. Ich sah Ihre Anzeige in der Zeitung.
   a) ☐ I have seen your advertisement in the newspaper.
   b) ☐ I sawn your advertisement in the newspaper.
   c) ☐ I saw your advertisement in the newspaper.

5. Mr Hudson wohnt seit 1990 in der Baker Street.
   a) ☐ Mr Hudson has lived in Baker Street since 1990.
   b) ☐ Mr Hudson is living in Baker Street since 1990.
   c) ☐ Mr Baker lives in Baker Street since 1990.

6. Hudson hat Griechenland vor 2 Jahren besucht.
   a) ☐ He was in Greece since two years.
   b) ☐ He went to Greece two years ago.
   c) ☐ He has been to Greece two years ago.

Elvira rummaged in her fashionable bag, which without doubt had cost most of Hudson's monthly salary. On the front of it, shone the name of a designer in golden letters, which Hudson could not even pronounce.
At long last, Elvira took a piece of paper out of her bag and unfolded it carefully. "This is a list of the Egyptian artifacts that have been stolen over the last few months."
Hudson bent over and looked at the list.
A broker in Soho had had a golden statue of the cat goddess stolen. A widow in Switzerland had informed the police that a golden sceptre of an Egyptian prince had gone missing. An American film producer, whose name Hudson had vaguely heard of, had been robbed of an Egyptian death mask.
And that was only the beginning of the list.

ÜBUNG 31 !

Übung 31: Übersetzen Sie die Sätze im Konditional!

1. Er würde es nie zugeben, dass er Elvira mochte.

____

2. Das Tatmotiv würde einen Hinweis auf den Dieb geben.

____

3. Inspector Hudson würde stolz auf sie sein.

____

4. Er würde herausfinden, wer die Mumie gestohlen hat.

____

5. Es war mehr Geld, als er jemals beim Yard verdienen würde.

____

6. Er würde mit ihr zusammenarbeiten.

____

7. Aber Sir Reginald würde nie etwas davon erfahren.

____

"Astonishing," murmured Hudson. "A serial thief, who only steals Egyptian antiquities."
"Exactly. And many of them were insured by my company."
"And you think the same thief stole the mummy from the museum?"
"I'm convinced of it, James."
"And why do you think that precisely the mummy theft will lead us to the criminal?"
"It's very simple, James," smiled Elvira, "because you have been assigned to the case."

Übung 32: Geben Sie den Komparativ und den Superlativ der folgenden Adjektive an!

1. happy ______________ ______________

2. good ______________ ______________

3. young ____________ ____________

4. beautiful ____________ ____________

5. bad ____________ ____________

6. comfortable ____________ ____________

7. busy ____________ ____________

8. patient ____________ ____________

9. polite ____________ ____________

10. far ____________ ____________

James Hudson could not help but feel flattered.

Perhaps that was the reason, he took a list out of his pocket, although it went strictly against the rules.

"Today I was given this list," said Hudson and showed Elvira the printed sheet.

"It looks like the thief sneaked into the museum without having to force open a door. Therefore it is obvious that he or she had a key … an 'access card'. This is a list of the people who have such a card. From the caretaker to the museum manager."

"But there are dozens!" gasped Elvira.

Hudson nodded his head frustrated.

"I'm afraid so. And any one of them could be the thief. Apart from the fact that one of these cards might have been stolen. However, today I saw the surveillance video of the theft and –"

"A video? That means the thief was filmed?" Elvira interrupted him. Hudson nodded.

"Yes and no. He was unrecognizable. But he was so sure of himself in the museum room, that he must have known the museum inside out."

Übung 33: Vervollständigen Sie die Sätze mit ***anything, nothing, nobody, anywhere, anybody!***

ÜBUNG 33 !

1. I don't want ____________ to drink. I'm not thirsty.
2. The museum was completely empty. ____________ was in it.
3. What did you buy? ____________. There wasn't ____________ I liked.
4. Have you seen my watch? I can't find it ____________.
5. There was complete silence in the room. ____________ said ____________.
6. She told ____________ about her plans.
7. She wasn't afraid of ____________.

"Well," sighed Elvira, "that reduces the number of suspects to a couple of dozen."
"Police work is hard work," said Hudson nearly joyfully. With a list full of suspects he was right in his element.

Übung 34: Unterstreichen Sie Hudsons Gedanken!

ÜBUNG 34 !

"I have a proposal. Why don't you check if the stolen goods on your list have anything in common. And I'll deal with my list."
"Does that mean we're working together, James?"
Her face broke into a wide smile.
Well, what should he do, thought Hudson. After all, if it hadn't been for Elvira, he might never have heard about the other thefts.

It was only fair to let her take part in the investigation.
Sir Reginald must never know of it, though.
"Sure, as long as you don't get in my way, Elvira."
"Fantastic!" shouted Elvira for joy.
"If you can excuse me, I have to go to my office and report to Sir Reginald."
"Of course, James. Give my regards to the old bulldog."
James could not stop himself from smiling, as he looked around for the waiter.
"Leave it, James," said Elvira. "Your tea's on me. I wanted to order something else anyway."
"Thanks for the invitation, Elvira."
"You're welcome, James. Here's to our collaboration."
"Yes, … our collaboration," replied James.
Hopefully he would not regret this decision. He stood up and went towards the door.

The cold drizzle hit his face.
Behind him he heard Elvira ordering yet another coffee.
Hudson drove his Bentley into the parking place behind the building of New Scotland Yard. He made sure that he had put away the list of card holders. Then he went into the building through the back entrance. He took the lift up to the third floor where Sir Reginald had his office.
He went down the passageway and straightened his tie before knocking on the door.
Instead of the expected 'come in', the door was torn open. Sir Reginald stood before him panting like a bulldog in a tweed jacket.
"Hudson," he growled, "there you are at last. I've been trying to get hold of you the whole morning. Sooner or later you'll have to get a mobile phone!"

Übung 35: Welche Gegenteile gehören zusammen? Setzen Sie die richtige Nummer ein!

1. straight	☐ boiling
2. back	☐ poor
3. wealthy	☐ reserved
4. young	☐ crooked
5. freezing	☐ lazy
6. hard-working	☐ cry
7. laugh	☐ elderly
8. outgoing	☐ front
9. black	☐ decrease
10. grow	☐ angel
11. tumult	☐ often
12. devil	☐ identical
13. broken	☐ intact
14. diverse	☐ white
15. seldom	☐ calm

God forbid, thought Hudson and followed his superior with surprise.
"What's wrong, Sir Reginald?" he enquired.
"What's wrong. Hell's broken loose! And all because of a damned mummy!"
Hudson followed the man in a hurry. Both came to a room with a large door.
'Conference room' were the words written over it.
"In the conference room, sir?" asked Hudson surprised. "Have we set up a special investigation panel?"
"Special investigation panel," growled Sir Reginald. "I suppose you could also call it that."

Übung 36: Welches Wort gehört in die Lücke!
(charge, manslaughter, sentence, defence, guilty, killed, stole)

1. You'll be OK. Get a good ____________ lawyer.
2. If the police arrest you they ____________ you with a crime.
3. The charge of murder was reduced to ____________.
4. Because of good behaviour their ____________ was reduced by a year and a half.
5. The thief ____________ the Crown Jewels from the Tower Bridge.
6. She ____________ her husband with a knife while he was asleep.
7. The court found him ____________ of murder.

Sir Reginald opened the door and nearly pushed Hudson into the room.
The inspector closed his eyes blindly. He was greeted by a storm of flashes. At least two dozen reporters jumped up from their places armed with cameras and notebooks.
Sir Reginald pulled poor Hudson to the speaker's desk.
"Our special investigator, Inspector James Hudson, is at your disposal for any questions, ladies and gentlemen. Fire away!"
Another series of flashes was followed by a confused wave of questions.
"Good luck, my friend!" Sir Reginald growled in Hudson's ear. And then he took off hurriedly towards the door.
"Are you already on the tracks of the mummy thief?" asked a fat reporter with a sweaty shirt.

"Do you think Tut-Enk-Ra's curse has anything to do with this?" shouted a lady with pink make-up.
"Is it all a publicity gag by the British Museum?" asked a thin man who obviously wrote for a serious newspaper.
The inspector swallowed.
"Hmm, please one after the other, ladies and gentlemen. I'll answer all your questions one after the other if possible."

Übung 37: Unterstreichen Sie die Verben im Past Perfect und Past Perfect Continuous!

ÜBUNG 37

A pimply young man with a "Star-Trek" T-shirt waved wildly in the air with his pencil.
"Does the mummy theft have anything to do with the latest corn circle sightings?" he asked in a shrill voice.
Inspector Hudson sighed and wished he had not answered the phone that morning.
It was a nightmare.

The dead silence around Elvira was driving her mad.
She had been sitting in this boring library for an hour studying all types of books on Egyptian art.
She had laid down the list of all the stolen relics next to the pile of books. She had been busy for the last hour gathering information and analysing the story of each piece.
If it carried on like this she would soon be able to take part in a quiz transmission on Egyptian culture. And there were still a lot of empty spaces on her list.
She still hadn't come across anything important. The stolen pieces were more or less valuable; some of the policy holders had

cheated a little on the value of their items. The company would be glad about that, but all in all, this terribly boring research had not led her anywhere.
The next item on her list was a scarab pendant which had been stolen from an opera singer.

ÜBUNG 38 !

*Übung 38: In welchem der folgenden Sätze muss ein Artikel stehen? (**the**, **a**, **an** oder nichts)*

1. Elvira is going on ____________ holiday.
2. The police are still looking for ____________ evidence.
3. This fingerprint is ____________ proof that he did it.
4. Mr Hudson lives in ____________ city of London.
5. Miss Paddington goes to ____________ church on Sunday.
6. Lord Winterbutton is ____________ member of the 'Egyptian Society'.
7. James is looking forward to seeing ____________ good old Elvira again.

Elvira turned over the pages of the next volume and followed the index at the end of the book with her forefinger.
The pendant – a copy of a dung-beetle, revolting – was actually described in the book.
Bored to tears, the insurance agent skimmed through all the information she could find about the relic.
Age, function, estimated value, site of finding.
Blah, blah, blah.

Suddenly, she stopped short, and turned back the page.
These Egyptian names were real tongue twisters, but she had not been mistaken. Elvira picked up her list. For each stolen relic she had taken notes which she was comparing.
… it was right …
She closed the thick volume triumphantly.
A loud thump resounded through the library. A few visitors looked at her irritated. But Elvira took no notice whatsoever.
Inspector Hudson would be proud of her.
Regardless of the fact she was in a library, she picked up her mobile to phone him.
Then she remembered that the charming, old-fashioned man did not own one.
Elvira folded up her list and left the library without putting away the books she had consulted.
An elderly lady at a table nearby shook her head.

Übung 39: Beantworten Sie die Fragen zum Text!

ÜBUNG 39 !

1. Why had Sir Reginald been looking for Hudson all morning?

____

____

2. What was Elvira doing at the library?

____

____

3. Why do you think Hudson does not own a mobile phone?

____

____

James Hudson sat exhausted in his office. He felt as if he had just fought with a pack of hyenas. What had happened to the good old British press?

The reporters had tortured him for two hours with stupid questions. Two hours which he could have easily made better use of, if he had looked for clues.

Übung 40: Verbinden Sie die Bezeichnung der Tierarten mit dem richtigen 'collective noun'! Setzen Sie die Ziffer in das Kästchen!

1. swarm	☐ hyenas
2. pack	☐ geese
3. flight	☐ wolves
4. herd	☐ fish
5. pack	☐ birds
6. school	☐ bees
7. gaggle	☐ cattle

He was frustrated as he looked at the list of card owners who had free access to the British Museum. The list ranged from 'A' for Atwood, animal embalmer, to 'Z' such as Zin-Yang Wo, caretaker of the Chinese section.

Hopefully Elvira was having more luck, thought the inspector to himself.

And she was!

At that very moment the door opened and Elvira Elliot walked into the room, naturally without knocking.

"Elvira," exclaimed Hudson, "I was just thinking of you at the moment!"

"How nice, I'm happy to hear that," she laughed.

"I've had a terrible morning," sighed Hudson thinking of the frightfully noisy reporters.
"Oh, so have I," said Elvira recalling the terribly boring and silent library.
"Anyway," she continued, "I've come across something very interesting."
"Fire away!" said the inspector looking curiously at the scribbled piece of paper that Elvira was waving in the air.
Elvira looked around Hudson's tiny little office and sceptically observed the bare walls and the miserable cactuses, growing on the window sill.

Übung 41: Setzen Sie die Verben in der richtigen Zeitform ein!

Then she (1. pull) ______ up a chair and (2. sit) ______ next to Hudson.
The inspector (3. can) __________ smell her fruity perfume. He had to ask her what it was when the opportunity came up. In all probability it had an exotic name and (4. be) ______________ very expensive.
Then his attention focussed once more on important things. Elvira moved a couple of files aside and smoothed the sheet of paper on the desk.
"Well," she began, "I spent hours looking for information concerning the stolen Egyptian items. It was so boring.

But while I (5. do) ____________________ it I (6. come across) __________ something very interesting."

The inspector looked at her in suspense.

Elvira (7. take) _______ a long pause. She seemed to be enjoying the suspense.

"Over the last few months, various Egyptian relics (8. steal + passive) __________________________________ all over the world.

In England, Europe, the USA and even in Australia. And this list only contains the items which were reported missing."
"And?" asked Hudson impatiently.
"All the stolen objects have one thing in common. Not only did they all come from the same dynasty, but they were also all found in the same tomb chamber. And guess which one?"
Hudson hardly needed to guess.
"In Tut-Ench-Ra's tomb chamber!" he exclaimed.
"In the last resting place of the prince, whose mummy was removed last night. Exactly."
Hudson fell back in his chair.
That was more than a mere coincidence. Someone was after the ancient tomb treasures that were meant to accompany the prince on his journey to the other world. And had then taken the good old boy too.
Strange, very strange indeed!
All the more of a case for him.
He could feel his hunting fever rising. But he had to control it. This case, like any other, needed presence of mind and cool deduction.

Übung 42: Bilden Sie Sätze mit dem Komparativ!

Beispiel: The Thames/The Nile
The Nile is longer than the Thames.

1. Bentley/Ford (expensive)

____

2. clock/watch (big)

____

3. pyramid/sphinx (high)

____

4. village/town (large)

____

5. pond/lake (deep)

____

6. bush/tree (tall)

____

7. England/Germany (big)

____

Elvira looked at him expectantly.
"Fantastic work, Elvira. Absolutely super," said Hudson and proudly looked at her.
The insurance agent laughed happily.

"But what do we do now?" she asked.

"Good question," replied Hudson.

He meditated. If the thief was so interested in the old Egyptian prince, the mummy must have had something interesting itself. They needed more information. And this is why they had – and Scotland Yard had – a very good source of information.

The Internet.

"Let's see if the Web knows anything about our prince," said Hudson turning on the computer.

Of course, it wasn't the latest version, and the old box needed a few minutes before the homepage was loaded.

In the meantime, Hudson had had enough time to brew some tea and offer Elvira a cup.

ÜBUNG 43 !

Übung 43: Setzen Sie die Präpositionen ein!

1. The thief broke __________ the building and stole the painting.
2. While surfing on the Web, I came __________ some interesting information.
3. It didn't take him long to find __________ who the thief was.
4. Somebody was __________ all the relics found in the tomb.
5. The police are looking __________ a man with a limp.
6. Take good care __________ yourself!
7. Elvira has decided to give __________ drinking coffee.

The young woman was so excited, that she even gulped down the tea, without asking for coffee.

"I would never have thought you could use the Internet, James," she said dryly. "Isn't it too modern for you?"
"Well, I must admit that, at first, I was a bit at loss with it, but since then it has become an irreplaceable source of information for me."
Actually the inspector enjoyed surfing on the Web in his little free time, searching for up-to-date news on criminal investigation or reading reports on historical cases.
The computer's modem made a shrill noise and the connection had been made. Hudson had requested a permanent line months before, but the bureaucracy at the Yard was as slow as any other authority.
Especially when it meant spending money.
Hudson thought quickly and typed the name of Tut-Enk-Ra in the search bar of a search engine.
Both looked curiously at the screen.
Only seconds later a very long list with texts and websites containing the name of the prince appeared.
"Oh dear," cried Elvira. "Another endless list."

Übung 44: Schreiben Sie die Zahlen in Buchstaben!

1. 26 ______________________
2. 2nd ______________________
3. 1st ______________________
4. 30th ______________________
5. $^{1}/_{2}$ ______________________
6. 1933 ______________________

ÜBUNG 44 !

7. 853000 ____________________

8. 5.78 ____________________

9. $^3/_4$ ____________________

"Don't worry, Elvira. It looks worse than it actually is."
In fact, many entries were only references to online editions of various newspapers which contained articles on the missing mummy.
A quarter of an hour and two cups of tea later, Hudson and Elvira had found a very interesting source. It was the homepage of the 'Egyptian Society', of an exclusive London-based club, founded by the descendants of the members of old expeditions and Egyptologists.

ÜBUNG 45 !

Übung 45: Unterstreichen Sie all die Verben, die mit dem Sprechen zu tun haben!

"What a club of old gentlemen," murmured Elvira, when she saw a group photo of the club members. "And in all probability women aren't even allowed in the club."
"Ah, how peaceful it must be," said the inspector jokingly.
"James!" exclaimed Elvira laughing and threatened him with a rolled up file.
"I'm sorry, Elvira. But this 'Egyptian Society' looks to me like a very conservative hangout. And look here – there's a link to information concerning Tut-Enk-Ra!"
"Click it!" cried Elvira very excited.
The inspector moved the cursor on the name of the old Pharaoh and pressed the mouse button. Seconds later a new page opened.

A scanned, yellowed photo was displayed. It showed a man in his thirties, standing proudly in front of the entrance to an Egyptian tomb chamber.

The large metal door behind him had been broken open with rudimentary tools. The methods used by archaeologists then were rather basic, thought Hudson.

"Who is this good-looking chap?" asked Elvira.

Hudson read the caption underneath.

"Lord Douglas Winterbutton, discoverer of Tut-Enk-Ra's tomb chamber, 1903"

By the looks of it, the lord had not hesitated at all before breaking into the Pharaoh's tomb.

"Rather extreme. But the fellow isn't bad looking at all."

Hudson had to admit that Lord Winterbutton had a really attractive face. If he had not been an archaeologist, he could have easily made a career as a film star. But that was not fitting for a lord. Not in those days.

Übung 46: Welche Wörter gehören in die Lücke?
(still, yet, any more/any longer, no longer)

ÜBUNG 46 !

1. It's 10 pm and Hudson is ____________ at work.
2. Has it stopped drizzling ____________?
3. She ____________ hasn't written to me.
4. Mr Johnson doesn't work here __________. He left a week ago.
5. He has been promoted. He is ____________ an inspector.
6. Harry lost his job last year and he is __________ unemployed.

Hudson cleared his throat and read the short text under the photo out loud.

"After the expedition was nearly declared a fiasco, Lord Douglas Winterbutton discovered by chance in 1903 the long sought tomb of the Pharaoh Tut-Enk-Ra.
Most of the relics found inside the chamber are privately owned, mainly by the Winterbutton family.
The mummy of the Pharaoh was soon donated to the British Museum."

"How generous," sneered Elvira. "They took the treasures home and donated the plundered mummy to the British Museum in London."
Hudson nodded. "That's how things went then. The British Empire considered nearly the whole world as its treasure chamber. Thank goodness things have changed since then."
"Yes, and …," Elvira wanted to add her opinion, but she noticed that Hudson was too busy reading her list.
"What are you looking for, James?" she asked.
James answered without looking up.
"Please see if Lord Winterbutton is on my list," said Hudson with a thoughtful glance."
"Sure," Elvira replied and skimmed through the list.
"Yes, here he is," she said a few seconds later. "Lord Stephen Winterbutton is a member of the museum's board of directors and has an access card."
"Interesting," murmured Hudson. "And … you're sure, he's not on your list."
Elvira looked at him questioningly.

Übung 47: Welches Verb gehört zu welchem Objekt? Setzen Sie die richtige Ziffer ein!

1.	fill in	☐ clothes in a shop
2.	put away	☐ children
3.	sort out	☐ information
4.	find out	☐ a new idea
5.	try on	☐ a mess
6.	try out	☐ clothes in a cupboard
7.	bring up	☐ a form
8.	take back	☐ a meeting to another time
9.	put off	☐ something you don't want
10.	clear up	☐ a fire
11.	put out	☐ a problem

"That could mean, my dear, that we have our first lead."
Elvira shrugged her shoulders.
"I don't understand. There's nothing concerning Lord Winterbutton."

Übung 48: Lesen Sie weiter und finden Sie ein sinnvolles Synonym!

"Exactly," (1. smiled) ____________ Hudson. "Just think. All the stolen items come from Tut-Enk-Ra's death chamber. According to the Internet, Lord Winterbutton (2. owns) ____________ one of the largest collections of the Pharaoh's (3. antiquities) ____________."

"And … yet, none of his items have been reported missing,"

exclaimed Elvira pensively. “Are you sure?”

“Yes. If the thief is only after treasures from Tut-Enk-Ra’s (4. tomb) ______________, then you’d think that he would have raided the largest existing collection.”

“Perhaps the (5. aristocrat’s) ____________________ house is too well secured,” suggested Elvira. “Or the thief is keeping the best items for last.”

Hudson rubbed his chin thoughtfully. “But there is another possibility. Lord Winterbutton is after all one of the people who have an access card. And therefore is also a suspect. Of course it could all be a (6. coincidence) __________ – but I don’t believe in coincidences. Not in such big ones, anyway.”

Elvira (7. exhaled) __________ sharply.

“Do you mean that Lord Winterbutton has set his heart on completing his collection? Legally or illegally?”

Hudson shrugged his shoulders.

“Maybe, Elvira. There’s no proof, but Lord Winterbutton is certainly at the top of the list of the people whom we need to speak to.”

“Another list,” sighed Elvira. However, she could not hide her thirst for action.

Inspector Hudson picked up the phone and dialled the information number to get Lord Winterbutton’s number.

The aristocrat lived in a villa not far from the old and famous Tower of London.

Übung 49: Welche Relativpronomen gehören in die Lücke? Oder bleiben Lücken leer?

1. I received a phone-call this morning ____________ really upset me.
2. I recently visited the town ____________ Al Capone was born.
3. Apparently she'd lost all her money gambling, ____________ really annoyed him.
4. The people ____________ used to live next-door have moved to Scotland.
5. Tom, ________________ parents live in London, is Hudson's colleague.
6. She told me a story ____________ I found hard to believe.
7. The year ____________ I was born, man went to the moon.
8. Miss Paddington cooked a meal ____________ tasted delicious.

Hudson took down the number and dialled it, without taking any notice of Elvira who was amused by the old-fashioned telephone. It rang at least a dozen times, before someone picked up the receiver.

A nasal voice answered.

"Lord Winterbutton's residence."

The inspector smiled. He would have been surprised if the lord had answered the phone personally.

"Good afternoon," he said, "I would like to speak to Lord Winterbutton. My name is Inspector James Hudson from Scotland Yard."

Übung 50: Hat das englische Idiom wirklich die gleiche Bedeutung? Markieren Sie: richtig ✓ falsch –

1. to ape someone – jemanden nachäffen
2. to swallow the bitter pill – in den sauren Apfel beißen
3. to have a bee in one's bonnet – eine Eselsbrücke bauen
4. to be on tenterhooks – gespannt sein
5. to be hot on someone's trail – Blut und Wasser schwitzen
6. to be after something – es auf etwas abgesehen haben
7. the last resting place – die letzte Ruhestätte

At the other end there was a small pause. That was not unusual. Most people were surprised when an officer from the legendary London Metropolitan Police phoned them.

"May I hear why?" asked the voice at the other end at last.

"I would like to tell Lord Winterbutton personally. Is he available?"

"I'm sorry, sir. But the lord is in a club at the moment, in London City."

"Oh, and what club would that be, may I ask?"

The voice at the other end answered: "Lord Winterbutton is at the Egyptian Society at the moment. Shall I give him a message when he comes home, sir?"

"That won't be necessary," replied Hudson. "I think we'll look for Lord Winterbutton at the club. May I ask with whom I have had the pleasure of speaking?"

"Of course, sir. My name is George and I'm Lord Winterbutton's butler."

"I thought so. Have a good day, sir."

Hudson put the receiver down. Elvira had listened to the conversation on the loudspeaker. She threw back her head and held her nose, so that her voice sounded like the nasal sound of the butler's. "I'm George the butler of the lord!" She had to laugh. "Oh dear, what a snob."

Übung 51: Geben Sie die richtigen Verbformen (im Passiv oder Aktiv) an!

ÜBUNG 51 !

New York police (1. announce) ____________ just ____________ that five paintings by Picasso (2. steal) ____________ from the Guggenheim Museum. The paintings (3. value) ____________ by experts at 5 million dollars. Police believe that they (4. take) ____________ early on Saturday evening, but for some reason the museums burglar alarm (5. not go off) ____________________. And the theft (6. not discover) ________________________ until Monday morning. No clues (7. find) ________________________ so far at the scene of the crime.

Hudson grinned and went to get his coat.
"Are you ready, Elvira? In all probability, the butler will have already informed his employer that Scotland Yard wants to speak to him. That is if the club allows modern means of communication like telephones."
But Elvira was looking at the computer screen.
She had found another interesting link on the homepage of the Egyptian Society.

Übung 52: Wählen Sie die richtige Form aus und kreuzen Sie sie an!

1. Hudson stopped
   a) ☐ to drink coffee when he was 30.
   b) ☐ drink coffee when he was 30.
   c) ☐ drinking coffee when he was 30.

2. Elvira and Hudson stopped
   a) ☐ having coffee in the café.
   b) ☐ to have coffee in the café.
   c) ☐ for having coffee in the café.

3. He tried
   a) ☐ to tell her the truth about the murder.
   b) ☐ to say her the truth about the murder.
   c) ☐ tell her truth about the murder.

4. The police let him
   a) ☐ to go after interrogating him.
   b) ☐ go after interrogating him.
   c) ☐ going after interrogating him.

5. She couldn't
   a) ☐ helping him on the case.
   b) ☐ help him on the case.
   c) ☐ to help him on the case.

6. Hudson enjoyed
   a) ☐ to work for Scotland Yard.
   b) ☐ work for Scotland Yard.
   c) ☐ working for Scotland Yard.

7. Elvira said she wouldn't mind
   a) ☐ to stay in the car.
   b) ☐ staying in the car.
   c) ☐ stay in the car.

"Just a second, James. This could be very interesting. I'll just print it out quickly, if you don't mind. Since I'm not allowed to enter this boring club, I need something to read to kill time."
Elvira pressed the mouse button and the printer in the corner of the office began to rattle.
The doorkeeper of the 'Egyptian Society' was not particularly impressed by the Bentley's arrival in front of the club. Of course, during his years as a porter he had seen many Bentleys park there, but none of them had been as old as this one.

Übung 53: Unterstreichen Sie die direkte Rede!

Inspector Hudson rolled down the window and smiled when he saw the porter's startled look.
"Good afternoon, old chap," he called, "where can I park my car, please?"
The porter had quickly recovered.
"I'm sorry sir, the club and its parking places are for members only."
"Arrogant pig!" whispered Elvira from the passenger seat. Hudson ignored her comment. He reached into the pocket of his coat and took out his official badge.
"I don't have a member's card, but perhaps this will open the door to your respectable rooms."
The porter swallowed hard.

"Scotland Yard? I'm very sorry, sir. I didn't know. You may park directly behind the building in the guests' parking place."
The inspector thanked the man and drove his car around the old Victorian building.
As promised, the building's courtyard housed a row of wide parking places for guests. Obviously most of the visitors came in wide limousines.
"Now, Elvira," said Hudson regretfully, "I'm afraid the authority of my badge is not enough to get you into the club as well."

ÜBUNG 54 !

Übung 54: Verwandeln Sie die Sätze in die indirekte Rede!

1. "Where can I park my car, please?" James asked where ______

   ____.

2. "I don't have a member's card." James said ______________

   ____.

3. "Perhaps my badge will let me in." James said ____________

   ____.

4. "You may park behind the building." The porter said _______

   ____.

5. "I'll read Lord Winterbutton's diary." Elvira said __________

   ____.

6. "You promised to rest, James." Miss Paddington said _______

   ____.

7. “What are you looking for James?” Elvira asked James ______

____.

Elvira shook her head.
“You must know that clubs which forbid women to enter are against the law, Mr Inspector?” she said smiling.
Hudson frowned. He believed he had just been informed of a relatively new constitutional ruling.
“Perhaps,” he said all the same, “there’s no point in getting the gentlemen angry. It would be much wiser if you simply waited for me in the car. It won’t take long.”
“Of course, James,” replied Elvira, “go alone. You’re right. Anyway, I brought myself something to read.”
The insurance agent picked up her hand bag where she had put the printed pages. Inspector Hudson said good-bye and got out the old Bentley.

Übung 55: Welches Wort passt in die Lücke?
(alibi, clue, evidence, red herring, inspector, suspects, witness)

1. A ____________ is something that helps to solve a mystery or problem.
2. A ____________ is a false lead that throws the investigator off track.
3. An ____________ is the proof of an accused person of not having been at the scene of crime.

4. A ____________ is a person who has personal knowledge about the crime.
5. An ____________ is an investigator or detective.
6. ____________ is something that tends to prove who committed the crime.
7. ____________ are people who appear to have a motive to have committed the crime.

Elvira sighed and took the printed Internet pages out of her bag. They were the facsimile of the diary of Sir Douglas Winterbutton, the discoverer of Tut-Enk-Ra's grave. She began reading the elegantly written daily entries. After a few minutes she had forgotten the rain pattering on the Bentley's windscreen.

ÜBUNG 56 !

Übung 56: Unterstreichen Sie die Synonyme der Wörter in Klammern! ***(surrender, fantasy, morale, hint, caught, puzzled, drugs, doubters)***

12th July 1903
"The heat is unbearable. I would do anything for a few drops of cool, English rain. We have been crossing the desert for days now, without even a trace of Tut-Enk-Ra's pyramid.
I'm starting to believe that the sceptics in London were right and that this mysterious Pharaoh is only a product of the imagination, a legend. A couple of the expedition members are already insisting we give up the search. But I don't want to give up yet."

13th July 1903

"The troop's spirits are getting lower and lower. Two of the carriers have picked up an unknown fever. Doctor Fauntleroy, the expedition's physician, is perplexed. None of the medication seems to be helping.

And I myself feel like giving up. But I do not want to give the sceptics in London that satisfaction."

14th July 1903

"What a day!

This morning, Achmed, our guide, came across a strange, pointed stone in the middle of the desert. At first, we did not give the finding much importance, but then my curiosity took over. I made the men dig up the stone, which to our surprise took longer and longer.

And then I realized that it wasn't just a stone in the desert, but the broken tip of a small pyramid, which had been covered by desert sand over the centuries.

Tut-Enk-Ra's Pyramid.

I've found it!"

Übung 57: Setzen Sie ***been*** *oder* ***gone*** *in die Lücke ein!*

ÜBUNG 57 !

1. "Where's Hudson?" "He's ____________ into the club."
2. Where has Elvira ____________ – she's so brown?
3. I've never ____________ to London, but I'd like to go.
4. "Are you going to the cinema this afternoon?" "No, I've already ____________."

5. "Where's Tom these days?" "Didn't you know? He's ______ ________ to another company."

6. "When's your holiday Elvira?" "I've already ____________. I went to Europe."

7. "Can I speak to Lord Winterbutton, please?" "I'm afraid he's __________ to the club. Can I take a message?"

15th July 1903
"It is very difficult for me to write. My hands are trembling for excitement and also because of the unknown fever which I have also caught.
But that doesn't matter now. This afternoon we found the entrance to the inside of the pyramid. A narrow passageway leads directly to the tomb which is closed by a metal door. The door is covered in hieroglyphs. But, luckily, our guide was able to decipher some of them.
It seems to be a warning. Whoever disturbs the Pharaoh's last resting place shall be put under a curse, which will afflict his children and his children's children.
What nonsense.
Naturally I broke down the door immediately. And I did not allow anyone to enter the grave before me.
Incredible treasures glowed in the light of my torch. I shall pack them up carefully and ship them to London.
My return home will be triumphant!
I can hardly wait to embrace my beloved Mary and to cover her with the ancient treasures like a queen!

But now I have to end today's entry. The doctor ordered me to rest, so that I may recover from the fever.
Tomorrow's another day."

ÜBUNG 58 !

Übung 58: Bilden Sie mit Hilfe eines Partizips aus zwei Sätzen einen!

1. I heard her. She whispered all through the night.
I heard her whispering all through the night.

2. Hudson sits in his bureau. He listens to the radio.

3. Elvira finds out a lot. She reads the books.

4. Miss Paddington came into the kitchen. She wanted to cook for dinner.

5. The man walks away. He looks a little pale.

Elvira put down the last page of the diary. What a story.
In the meantime, Inspector Hudson had entered the time-honoured rooms of the 'Egyptian Society'.
The distinct smell of leather chairs, old books and pipe smoke hit him.
This club was the quintessence of English tradition.
Hudson went into the entrance hall.

He was immediately greeted by a butler, who managed to cover the distance between them in record time.
"Can I help you?" he asked.
"Yes, actually," answered Hudson. "My name is Hudson, from Scotland Yard. I would like to speak to Lord Winterbutton."
"Of course, sir. But I'm not sure he's here. Please follow me to the club room."

ÜBUNG 59 !

Übung 59: Unterstreichen Sie alle Präpositionen mit lokaler Bedeutung!

"Thank you," replied Hudson and followed the uniformed man.
The entrance hall had been impressing enough, but this room was even more luxurious. An enormous Indian carpet stretched from one end of the room to the other. The walls were covered with oak book shelves holding without doubt thousands of books.
Hudson had seen city libraries with less volumes. All around the room there were very old and terribly comfortable-looking leather armchairs. Next to each one was a small table where an ashtray or a glass of sherry could be placed.
And despite the early hour, the club was already frequented by quite a few members.
There were thick clouds of smoke in the air.
A few visitors were sitting in the armchairs reading the newspaper, others were reading books or conversing in hushed tones.
Once in a while a hearty laugh rang through the room.

The butler asked Inspector Hudson to wait a moment.
Then he left to search for Lord Winterbutton.
Hudson watched amused as the butler carefully peered over

the armrests of the chairs to see who was behind the newspaper. He did not want to disturb the guests in any way.
Eventually he came back.
"I'm sorry sir. But it looks as if Lord Winterbutton is not present."
He looked as if he considered the circumstance as a personal defeat.

Übung 60: Unterstreichen Sie das passende Wort!

ÜBUNG 60 !

1. He wasted/earned all his money betting on the horses.
2. Elvira is very hard up/well-off. She's just bought herself a sports car.
3. If only Lord Winterbutton had left him something in his will/savings.
4. His grandfather keeps all his money in a cash dispenser/safe under the bed.
5. Hudson's salary/wages is paid into his bank account every month.
6. A penny is an English coin/currency.
7. I'm bankrupt/broke. Can you lend me a couple of pounds until the end of the month.

"Don't worry," said Hudson and was about to leave when an elderly man came up to him.
"Are you looking for the young Lord Winterbutton?" asked the man in a croaking voice.
Hudson looked at the old man. He was haggard and had a very pronounced hooked nose. A few wisps of white hair lay in a disorderly manner on an otherwise bald head. The man was so curved, he reminded Hudson of a giant question mark on legs.
"Well, yes," replied Hudson a little surprised.

The butler left with a slight bow. Hudson had a feeling that he was in a hurry to get away.

Übung 61: Verwandeln Sie das Adjektiv in ein Adverb!

1. perfect ____________________
2. careful ____________________
3. heavy ____________________
4. good ____________________
5. fast ____________________
6. hard ____________________
7. late ____________________

"Yes, the fellow is no longer here," the old man croaked.
"Yes, the butler has already told me so. I'll try coming again when Winterbutton is here."
"Good idea," said the old man, "but don't wait too long before paying him a visit, ha ha."
The old man's laugh sounded more like a crow.
Hudson frowned. "What do you mean by that?"
"Well," answered the old man with a nearly sorrowful gesture, "it's nearly Stephen's birthday. He's turning thirty-three, poor fellow."
Hudson shook his head irritated.
"I don't quite understand, Mister –?"
"Cornwall," said the man, "Ebenezer Cornwall."
Hudson shook the man's hand. His skin was very thin, but his handshake was surprisingly strong.

"Pleased to meet you, sir. My name is James Hudson, from Scotland Yard."
Mr Cornwall smiled.

Übung 62: Finden Sie das Gegenteil für die Wörter in Klammern!

"I see. From Scotland Yard. Stephen hasn't been up to mischief, has he. If you want to charge him with (1. nothing) __________, then you'd better (2. take your time) __________."

Mr Cornwall laughed in his ugly way again. A few of the other guests turned around surprised. The old man did not seem to notice. Another allusion, thought Hudson. What did this all mean.

It would be (3. worst) __________ to be (4. indirect) __________ __________ with the old man and ask him what he meant.

"Sir, would you be (5. rude) __________ enough to tell me exactly what you mean?"

Mr Cornwall studied Hudson.

"You don't know anything, do you?"

Then he said: "Ah, how could you? Here at the club everyone has heard the story. And I leave this place so (6. often) __________, I sometimes forget there's a (7. unreal) __________ world (8. inside) __________ with cable TV, notebooks, satellites and those small, cordless phones, uhhm, what are they called …?"

"Mobile phones," said Hudson laughing at the old man.

"Yes of course. Those little pests."

The inspector nodded in (9. disagreement) ___________. "I have to agree with you there. But you were telling me about what you meant with …"

The old man (10. put down) ___________ his bushy eyebrows.

"Was I? Oh yes. I go off track sometimes."

Hudson sighed. He hoped he would never need Mr Cornwall as a witness.
Mr Cornwall pointed at two free armchairs next to each other in the corner of the room.
"Let's sit down," he said, "my rheumatism is giving me trouble."
Hudson followed the old man to the armchairs, which not only looked comfortable.

ÜBUNG 63 !

Übung 63: Setzen Sie das richtige Adverb/Adjektiv in die Lücke ein! ***(hard, hardly, late, lately, good, well)***

1. Your writing is terrible. I can ___________ read it.
2. Elvira works very ___________.
3. How much did she eat? ___________ anything.
4. She speaks English very ___________.

5. The company's financial situation is not very ____________ at the moment.

6. Have you seen Tom ____________?

7. I think he was fired because he was always ________ for work.

Mr Cornwall waved at the butler. A few seconds later he brought a decanter of sherry and two glasses. Mr Cornwall obviously ordered this often.

The old man poured himself a glass and sipped it with pleasure.

"Ah, this invigorates heart and soul. Help yourself to one, old friend."

Hudson refused politely.

"No, thank you. It's a bit too early for me. No alcohol before sunset."

The old man replied: "Does that mean you stay thirsty in the summer?"

The inspector looked at his watch meaningfully. Elvira was still waiting outside in the car. And patience was not a virtue she possessed.

Hudson was afraid she would burst into the club any moment.

Mr Cornwall saw him do this and laughed.

Übung 64: Übersetzen Sie folgende Sätze!

ÜBUNG 64 !

1. Inzwischen hatte Hudson genug Zeit gehabt, um einen Tee zu kochen und Elvira eine Tasse zu servieren.

____

____

2. Lord Douglas Winterbutton entdeckte im Juli 1903 durch einen Zufall die Grabkammer des Pharaos Tut-Ench-Ra.

3. Es läutete mindestens ein Dutzend Mal, bevor jemand am anderen Ende der Leitung abhob.

4. Inspector Hudson verabschiedete sich und stieg aus dem Wagen.

5. Ein paar der anderen Gäste blickten sich überrascht um.

6. Mister Cornwall deutete auf zwei freie Sessel, die in einer Ecke des Saales beieinander standen.

7. Geduld war eine Tugend, die Elvira ganz sicher nicht besaß.

"I see. You're in a hurry. Of course. Can't keep crime waiting, can you? So what was I saying?"
"I'm not sure," answered Hudson patiently, "but you made some allusions in which you said that Lord Winterbutton might pass away soon."
"Oh yes." The old man seemed nearly pleased. He probably didn't find that many people to talk to at the club.
Then he cleared his throat and looked ahead to concentrate.
Hopefully, he wouldn't start from Adam and Eve thought Hudson. He thought of Elvira again sitting in the car.

Übung 65: Unterstreichen Sie die Verben!

ÜBUNG 65 !

"It all began in the summer of 1903," started Mr Cornwall. "At that time the British Empire was world power. Lord Douglas Winterbutton was heading an expedition which aimed at finding the grave of the legendary Tut-Enk-Ra. Nobody knew for sure then if the Pharaoh really had existed or if he was just a myth.
Many of his contemporaries thought he was a crazy man who would only obtain one thing with the expedition: to squander his family's considerable patrimony. And many regarded him as an irresponsible, since he was married to a beautiful woman who was expecting his child.
But the lord was very stubborn and took the chance. Such an expedition was a real adventure in those days. All the equipment had to be transported on camels and there were no satellite photos of the desert to help archaeologists find the tombs.

Anyhow, the expedition seemed to be an absolute fiasco. Winterbutton was on the point of becoming the laughingstock of the aristocracy, because he was chasing a ghost through the desert. But perhaps you already know how it ended. After many weeks the lord discovered the pyramid by chance.

Rash as he was, he broke down the door there and then. He ignored the curse that Tut-Enk-Ra was supposed to have made. Anyone who disturbed the Pharaoh's tomb would have to pay dearly for it. And so would his descendants."

"A veritable biblical curse," added Inspector Hudson.

"In any case. Foolish superstition, is what we'd call it today. And that's what Lord Winterbutton also thought. He had the whole tomb emptied and took the cache to his estate in England. Of course, that wasn't completely legal. But those were turbulent times and people had other things to worry about.

The Winterbutton family were anything but hard up and the little Egyptian adventure had not increased family's wealth particularly. At the time the Winterbuttons were one of the richest families in the country. Only later during the First World War were they forced to sell a few Egyptian relics to collectors from all over the world.

What a pity that Douglas Winterbutton did not benefit from it," said Mr Cornwall.

! ÜBUNG 66

Übung 66: Welches Wort ist das „schwarze Schaf"?

1. disease, fever, hunger, illness ____________
2. son, grandson, aunt, friend ____________
3. throat, dizzy, forehead, eyebrow ____________
4. whirlwind, tornado, hurricane, widow ____________

5. crow, penguin, sparrow, seagull ____________

6. bumper, review mirror, dashboard, dish ____________

7. story, narration, author, fable ____________

The old man cleared his throat and sipped some sherry.
"Excuse me, my throat is dry from this dusty story."
Mr Cornwall cleared his throat again and continued his narration. Or rather he wanted to continue but apparently had lost the thread.
"Hmm, where was I?" he asked the inspector.
"You were saying that Lord Winterbutton did not benefit from the treasures he found."
"That's right. It appears that Tut-Enk-Ra's curse was more than a trick to mislead superstitious tomb raiders. Shortly after opening the Pharaoh's tomb, Lord Winterbutton caught a mysterious fever which got worse every day. The expedition's doctor was powerless. Soon the aristocrat was but a shadow of his former self and he died during the journey home. Exactly on his thirty-third birthday. A few months later his widow bore a son who would never see his father."
The inspector nodded.

Übung 67: Welche Sätze sind richtig?
Markieren Sie: richtig ✓ falsch –

ÜBUNG 67 !

1. When Hudson entered the club a few visitors were sitting on stools speaking very loudly.
2. The descendants of Lord Winterbutton were his grandfather and his great grandfather.
3. Lord Winterbutton nearly gave up his search for the pyramid.

4. The expeditioners saw a cave in the desert which turned out to be the tomb.
5. The Winterbutton family was wealthy.
6. Lord Winterbutton entered the tomb after his helpers.
7. Hudson did not believe in the curse.

"What a tragic story, but surely a coincidence. In all likelihood, the lord had caught a tropical disease which would have killed him – with or without the curse."
The old man gave Hudson a penetrating look.
"It's possible, my friend, possible. But how do you explain then that his son, too, died on his thirty-third birthday and thirty-three years later his grandson?"
Hudson looked at the man silently. That was a very strong coincidence. And as he had told Elvira earlier on, he did not believe in coincidences. But, that would imply that he believed in a curse made thousands of years before by the Pharaoh.
And this thought pleased him even less.

ÜBUNG 68 !

Übung 68: Setzen Sie die Verben in der passenden Form (first conditional) ein!

1. If you (not live) *did not live* so far away, we *would visit* you more often.
2. Sir Arthur (not be) ____________ so fat, if he (eat) ____________ less.
3. If Hudson (not have to work) ____________ tomorrow, he (can

meet) ____________ Elvira.

4. This coffee (taste) ____________ better, if it (have) ____________ more sugar.

5. Hudson (know) ____________ who the thief is, if he (have) ____________ more clues.

6. If I (be) ____________ rich, I (live) ____________ near Hyde Park.

7. Hudson (buy) ____________ a new Bentley, if he (earn) ____________ more money.

8. If you (listen) ____________ to me, you (make) ____________ no mistakes.

Inspector Hudson thanked Mr Cornwall and stood up.
He noticed that he was a little dizzy, although he had not even touched the sherry.
Should he believe the old man's story? How could one Winterbutton die after the other on their thirty-third birthday because of a Pharaoh's curse? Or was there another darker explanation?
"Hmm," there was a little cough behind him, "excuse me, but I could not help overhearing your conversation."
Hudson turned around. A small rounded man in a dark suit stood before him. His jacket looked very expensive, but it pulled very dangerously across his big belly.
"Yes?" answered Hudson curiously. He had been so involved in Mr Cornwall's narration that he had not noticed the man at all. With his short legs and beak nose, the stranger reminded him of a penguin.

Übung 69: Steigern Sie die folgenden Adjektive!

1.	big	________	________
2.	nervous	________	________
3.	thirsty	________	________
4.	polite	________	________
5.	much	________	________
6.	good	________	________
7.	quiet	________	________
8.	far	________	________
9.	lucky	________	________
10.	careful	________	________

"My name is Arthur Cobblepot. Sir Arthur Cobblepot."
The man meaningfully stressed the word sir.
"I am, by the way, the Winterbutton family's lawyer. We have been representing the Winterbuttons for generations. May I ask why you are so interested in our client's story?"
"My name is James Hudson. Inspector James Hudson, from Scotland Yard. As you probably already know, this morning Tut-Enk-Ra's mummy was found missing from the British Museum. And as I have just found out, there is a special link between the Winterbutton family and the mummy."
Cobblepot nodded. "Yes, a tragic old story, in fact. But you can't really see a connection between the missing mummy and my client, Lord Stephen Winterbutton?"

The lawyer's question sounded more like a threat than a simple enquiry. Hudson jerked.

*Übung 70: Formulieren Sie Sätze mit dem Verb **wish**!*

1. Elvira can't give up drinking coffee. She wishes

   she could stop.

2. Hudson isn't here (and I need him). I wish

   ____

3. I live in London (and I hate London). I wish

   ____

4. Hudson has an old Bentley. He wishes

   ____

5. Lord Winterbutton is turning thirty-three soon. He wishes

   ____

6. Sir Cobblepot is short and fat. He wishes

   ____

7. I wish I (know) ____________________ how this book ends.

"Of course not," said the inspector. "But, after all, many of Tut-Enk-Ra's relics are owned by the Winterbuttons. Therefore I would like to consult Lord Winterbutton, for his expert advice."
The lawyer gave Hudson a penetrating look with his bird eyes.
"I see. I'm not sure if it is the right time. Lord Stephen is not

feeling very well at the moment. I saw him a little while ago and he looked rather unwell."

A croaking laugh came from the leather armchair next to Hudson. Mr Cornwall was watching the lawyer.

"He isn't feeling well, is he? So soon before his thirty-third birthday? What a coincidence. I told you inspector!"

Sir Arthur looked at the old man annoyed. "Please mind your own business, Cornwall. You should be ashamed of yourself for telling such old wives' tales."

For a moment Hudson feared the two men would fly at each other. The old crow against the fat penguin. What a scene. But the old man's reaction was only to laugh and to sip his sherry.

The lawyer shook his head, took a business card out of his pocket and gave it to the inspector.

Übung 71: Welches Wort hat die stärkere Bedeutung? Kreuzen Sie an!

1.	☐ angry	☐ annoyed
2.	☐ smile	☐ beam
3.	☐ hot	☐ boiling
4.	☐ exhausted	☐ tired
5.	☐ speak	☐ shout
6.	☐ terrified	☐ afraid
7.	☐ discuss	☐ argue

"Here is my card. As I said, my family's firm represents the Winterbuttons in all legal matters. Furthermore we are also their estate administrators. If you want to speak to Lord Winterbutton, I have to ask you to contact me first."

"Of course sir. I'll contact you in the next few days."
"Thank you, inspector, and have a nice day."
Having said this, Sir Arthur turned and left the room.
He waggled just like a penguin, thought Hudson amused.
But his smile did not last long. Hudson recalled what Cobblepot had said: it seemed that the present Lord Winterbutton was also ill. Shortly before his thirty-third birthday.
The whole story was becoming more and more mysterious.

Miss Paddington put a steaming cup of tea on the table in front of Hudson. "Thanks a lot," said Hudson smiling.
"You looked exhausted, James," said Miss Paddington, "a nice cup of Earl Grey is just what you need."
Hudson nodded. He really was tired. His planned 'day off' had turned out to be the most tiring day of the week. After his conversation with Cobblepot and Mr Cornwall, he had gone back to his car where Elvira was waiting impatiently. Last of all, he had accompanied the young insurance agent home. On the way there, the two had exchanged their stories. Elvira told Hudson of the former Lord Winterbutton's diary and Hudson completed the story with the information he had gathered from Mr Cornwall. Then he had left Elvira at her flat and had gone immediately home.

Übung 72: Finden und unterstreichen Sie die Synonyme der Wörter in Klammern! ***(thin, smiling, appreciatively, lounge, start again, presently, hollow)***

! ÜBUNG 72

He had worked enough for today.
"Shall I prepare you a couple of sandwiches, James?" asked Miss Paddington. "You probably haven't eaten anything the whole day.

You'll become skin and bones."
James thought about it. He had, in fact, forgotten to eat today. And only now that Miss Paddington had mentioned it, did he feel how empty his stomach was.
"Oh that would be so nice of you, my dear," he said gratefully.
Beaming, his housekeeper left the living room. Before long he heard the lady pottering about in the kitchen. He closed his eyes sleepily. And relaxing his shoulders, resumed the game he had been playing in the early morning.

He tried to guess what Miss Paddington was doing from the noises she made. A soft plucking noise indicated that she was preparing the lettuce leaves. Then there was the banging of the bread box, followed by the rhythmic noise of a knife-blade on wood. She was probably slicing the onions or tomatoes. Hudson's mouth watered. At least the day would have a peaceful finale. He breathed in deeply and felt pleasantly tired. But, then the doorbell rang. Hudson jumped out of his chair. In the kitchen Miss Paddington dropped the knife from the fright she got. "Who can it be so late in the evening?" she called. "People simply don't have good manners any more!" The inspector took a deep breath while Miss Paddington went to the door.

ÜBUNG 73 !

Übung 73: Verbinden Sie die Wörter, um Komposita zu bilden! Setzen Sie die richtige Ziffer ein!

1. driving	☐ estate
2. steering	☐ glasses
3. insurance	☐ card
4. air	☐ licence
5. birthday	☐ lights

6. motor	☐ agent
7. country	☐ port
8. sun	☐ way
9. head	☐ wheel

“It is not good manners to ring on somebody’s door so late!” he heard her say in the entrance.

But then her tone changed and became friendlier all of a sudden.

“Oh it’s you. That’s another matter. Please come in deary!”

The inspector was curious. “It’s you”? “Deary”?

Who could it be?

A few seconds later his question was answered.

Elvira Elliot stormed into the room, as excited and animated as usual.

Übung 74: Übersetzen Sie die Sätze!
Achten Sie dabei auf die Modalverben!

1. Er musste ziemlich oft ins Ausland fahren.

____

2. Die Familie Winterbutton hatte Pech gehabt.

____

3. Der Dieb muss es getan haben.

____

4. Hudson darf im Dienst nicht trinken.

____

"James!" she shouted, without bothering to say hello. "Are you ready?"
"Ready? For what? And a good evening to you too!"
Elvira waved her hand.
"OK, OK, good evening. Come on, it's already late."
The inspector shook his head.
"But, what is wrong?"
"Well, you don't want to idle away the evening, do you? While the mummy is up to its tricks. Or at least its curse is. I thought we could go to Lord Winterbutton and see how the fellow is."
"At this hour?" asked Hudson. "By the time we get there it'll be midnight!"
"All the better," replied Elvira. "Surprise visits have the best results."
The inspector rolled his eyes and sighed. It was no good contradicting Elvira. It would be like trying to stop a whirlwind. James got up from his armchair and went to get his coat.

ÜBUNG 75 !

Übung 75: Unterstreichen Sie Adverbien and Adjektive!

Inspector Hudson fastened his seat-belt carefully.
Elvira raced through the bends on the country road, without ever taking her foot off the accelerator. The centrifugal force pushed Hudson against the passenger's door. It was like being on a roller coaster.
"Could you please drive a little more slowly, Elvira?" he said gruffly.
Elvira shook her head. "I'm not a fast driver, James, but a sporty one."
"Then please be unsporty."

The insurance agent laughed and changed into a slower gear. "As you wish, James."

The inspector breathed out. Luckily Winterbutton's estate was not far away and they would probably get there safe and sound. Elvira had chosen the wrong profession. She should have been a racing driver. She took the next curve at a more moderate pace.

"Do you really believe there's a curse, James?" she asked, looking at him curiously. Hudson pointed at the road.

"I would appreciate it if you kept your eyes on the road. And no, I don't believe in supernatural curses, black magic and the likes."

Übung 76: Setzen Sie die Verben in der passenden Verbform ein.

ÜBUNG 76 !

1. If Hudson *had known* Sir Reginald was on the phone, he (not answer) ________________.
2. If Elvira (not drive) ________________ so fast, Hudson (not get) ________________ car sick.
3. If Lord Winterbutton (give) ________________ them an appointment, they (not go) ________________ to his home so late.
4. If Sir Douglas Winterbutton (be) ________________ poor, he (not go) ________________ on the expedition.
5. If Elvira (not follow) ________________ Hudson, he (not find out) ________________ about the other thefts.

6. If Sir Douglas Winterbutton (not go) _______________ to the desert, he (not die) _______________ of a fever.

"But it can't be a coincidence that all the Winterbuttons die on their thirty-third birthday. There must be something behind it all."
"Exactly," agreed Hudson. "Something we are going to find out!"
"Perhaps Lord Winterbutton can help us."
"That's if he lets us in at this time of the night," replied the inspector and looked at the digital clock on the dashboard. It was already 11 o'clock.
"Oh, I'm sure he will," said Elvira in a strange undertone. She had something in her mind, thought Hudson to himself, and I don't want to know what it is.
"Tell me Elvira, do you have the pages from the diary with you?" he asked.
Elvira nodded.
"Yes, in the glove compartment."
Hudson opened the glove compartment and took the pages out.
"Will it bother your driving if I switch the light on?"
"Not at all. The road is straight from here on."
Hudson switched on the small light on the car ceiling and began to read.

ÜBUNG 77

! *Übung 77: Übersetzen Sie und tragen Sie den richtigen Buchstaben ein! Wie lautet das Lösungswort?*

1. ruinieren _ _ ☐ _

2. Prinz _ _ _ ☐ _ _

3. Gewalt □ _ _ _ _ _ _ _

4. Landsitz _ _ _ _ _ □

5. Verdächtiger _ _ □ _ _ _ _

6. Grab □ _ _ _

7. Zufall _ _ □ _ _ _ _ _ _ _ _

8. vernehmen _ _ _ _ _ _ _ □ _ _ _

9. Zeitungsjunge _ □ _ _ _ _ _ _

10. Nachkomme _ _ _ _ _ _ _ _ _ □

11. sterben _ □ _

12. Sprache _ □ _ _ _ _

13. Schmerz _ _ _ □

Lösung: _ _ _ _ _ _ _ _ _ _ _ _ _

Elvira had told him what she had read in the diary, but one thing had puzzled him. He soon found what he was looking for. Elvira was curious.

“So, James?”

James pointed at the road.

“I’ll tell you as soon as you look at the road.”

The inspector referred to a passage from the diary.

“Here it is. On the 13th of July Lord Winterbutton wrote about two carriers catching an unknown fever which the expedition’s doctor could not cure.”

“Yes, and?” asked Elvira, this time without taking her eyes off the road.

Übung 78: Setzen Sie die folgenden Wörter in die Lücke:
much, many, a lot, a lot of

1. When Lord Winterbutton caught the fever there wasn't ______ ______ his doctor could do.
2. __________ people believed that the family was under a curse.
3. Hudson has __________ work to catch up on.
4. __________ of his contemporaries thought he was a crazy man who would only obtain one thing with the expedition.
5. Hudson thought nothing __________ could happen to anyone looking for a five-thousand-year old mummy.
6. Miss Paddington had been his housekeeper for __________ years now.
7. Actually, Hudson liked Elvira __________.
8. Perhaps he could turn a couple of his cases into detective books and earn __________ money.
9. There's __________ to be done.

"And it was only a day later, on the 14th of July, that he came across the pyramid. Soon after that he fell ill, too. He probably had the same unknown fever that the carriers had."
Elvira nodded thoughtfully.
"You're right. But the carriers had the symptoms before they discovered the pyramid."

Übung 79: Setzen Sie die richtigen Konjunktionen ein!
(unless, only, but, before, too, then)

Hudson nodded.

"Supposing the cause of the fever was the same."

"… which is highly probable …"

"The mummy's curse had nothing to do with Lord Winterbutton's death. (1.) __________ the Pharaoh's curse started (2.) __________ Winterbutton disturbed his sleep."

"Exactly," agreed Hudson.

"(3.) __________ that doesn't explain the mysterious deaths of his son and his grandson exactly on their thirty-third birthday."

"We'll get to the bottom of that mystery, (4.) __________, Elvira." said Hudson optimistically.

The inspector sighed happily. That took a load off his mind. He would have found it difficult to come to terms with the possibility of a curse. Elvira slowed down and turned into a wide driveway which led to a country house. (5.) __________ the entrance hall and a room on the first floor had their lights on.

Elvira stopped the car next to a Jaguar parked in front of the entrance door.
"Here we are," she said, "and by the looks of it, Lord Winterbutton is here, too."

She got out of the car and looked at the residence.
Hudson did the same. The building was at least 200 years old and, even in the dark, it emanated an atmosphere of old upper-class wealth.
The two of them went to the entrance door.
Portal would have been a more appropriate term. And as could be expected, there was no ordinary door bell, but, instead, an old door-knocker in solid iron, in the shape of a sphinx's face.
Without hesitating Elvira grasped it and hammered energetically on the door.

ÜBUNG 80 !

*Übung 80: Geben Sie die richtigen Formen von **to go** an!*

1. einfache Gegenwart: ______________
2. Verlaufsform der Gegenwart: ______________
3. Einfache Vergangenheit: *he went*
4. Vergangenheit mit "used to": ______________
5. Verlaufsform der Vergangenheit: ______________
6. present perfect: ______________
7. Verlaufsform des present perfect: ______________
8. Plusquamperfekt: ______________
9. Verlaufsform des Plusquamperfekts: *he had been going*
10. Zukunft mit "going to": ______________

11. Zukunft mit “will”: ______________________

12. future perfect: ______________________

13. Verlaufsform des future perfect: ______________________

The knocks echoed through the dead silent house.
Despite the late hour, it took only a few seconds for some limping steps to be heard. A man in a butler’s uniform opened the door. He looked about forty, had short, dark brown hair and a very striking face. And for a butler, who probably never carried anything heavier than a silver tray, he had surprisingly wide shoulders.
“Can I help you?” he asked.
Inspector Hudson was about to say something, but Elvira beat him to it.
“Good evening sir, we would like to speak to Lord Winterbutton.”
“And may I ask who you are?” asked the butler without batting an eyelid.
Hudson cleared his throat.

Übung 81: Welche Synonyme gehören zusammen? Setzen Sie die richtige Ziffer ein!

ÜBUNG 81 !

1. ancient	☐ deceased
2. automobile	☐ ask
3. dead	☐ policeman
4. enquire	☐ car
5. cop	☐ bizarre
6. steal	☐ old
7. strange	☐ pinch
8. drink	☐ sip

"I think we spoke to each other on the phone. Inspector Hudson from Scotland Yard and Elvira Elliot. May we speak to the lord?"
The butler looked at them doubtfully.
Then he shook his head.
"I'm sorry, but Lord Winterbutton is not feeling very well. If you could leave your business cards, he will definitely get in touch with you."
Hudson sighed and gave the man his card and so did Elvira.
The butler took the cards and bade them a good night before shutting the door.
They could hear a bolt being slid into place.
"What an unfriendly man," said Elvira.

Übung 82: Setzen Sie die passende Verbform ein!

But James Hudson (1. not listen) ______________. He (2. to stare) ______________ at the closed door. Something about the butler (3. to ring) ______________ a bell. "James, (4. to be) ______________ everything all right?" asked Elvira. Hudson still (5. to take) ______________ no notice of her. He (6. to try) ______________ to concentrate on the butler.

Something wasn't right.

Then it struck like a bolt of lightning!

Of course!

It wasn't the butler's face which had caught his attention, but the sound of his footsteps as he (7. to come) ______________ to the door.

"The butler limps!" he exclaimed.
Elvira looked at him questioningly.
"Sorry?"
"Elvira, when the butler opened the door I heard his feet dragging."
Elvira still did not understand.
How could she? The inspector led her away from the door.
"I told you that I saw the surveillance tape at the museum this morning …"
"Yes?"
"Well the thief could not be identified, but he had a limp!"
"Like the butler!" cried Elvira excitedly. The inspector put his index finger to his lips. "Shhh!" he said as they returned to the car. "It could also be a coincidence, but there seem to be a few too many coincidences now. Lord Winterbutton is the grandson of the Tut-Enk-Ra's discoverer; he has access to the museum; he is the only person whose relics have not been stolen; and his butler limps just like the thief. I believe we are on the right track!"
"Great! At last, we are taking a step forward." Elvira started the engine and drove the car back on the country road.

Übung 83: Beantworten Sie die Fragen zum Text!

1. What made Hudson believe that the curse didn't have anything to do with Lord Douglas Winterbutton's death?

2. How many rooms in Lord Winterbutton's country estate had their lights on?

3. What madc thc butler seem to be a possible suspect?

4. What made Lord Winterbutton a very probable suspect?

5. Why didn't Lord Winterbutton speak to Hudson and Elvira?

But, to Hudson's great surprise, she stopped the car on the side of the road, switched off the engine and jumped out.
"Come on, James! We have no time to lose!"
The inspector looked at her inquiringly.
"What are you doing, Elvira?"
"Well what do you think? If his lordship won't receive us, then we'll invite ourselves in!"
Hudson could not believe his ears.
"D-do you want to break into the house?" he stuttered.
Elvira laughed. "Don't look so shocked. We'll just have a little look around. Come on!"
Without waiting for his answer, she disappeared into the darkness in the direction of the country house. The inspector sighed and followed her unwillingly. Perhaps, he could at least prevent her from getting into trouble.
"Elvira you can't do that," he whispered.
"Too late!"
Elvira Elliot had found an unfastened kitchen window at the back of the house and was pushing it open carefully.

Übung 84: Setzen Sie die richtige Person ein!
(he, she, Hudson, Elvira)

Before (1.) ______________ could do anything, (2.) ______________ had already slipped into the house. (3.) ______________ then stuck her head out of the window and grinned at him.

"Come in or do you want to take root there?"

(4.) ______________ sighed again. This was trespassing. And as an officer of law he was supposed to arrest Elvira not become her accomplice. But now it was too late.

(5.) ______________ looked around him – like a thief in the night – and climbed through the window.

Once inside, (6.) ______________ looked around.

The kitchen light was off, but the moonlight was streaming through the window. The room was larger than Hudson's lounge and furnished with ultramodern kitchen fittings.
"Not bad," whispered Elvira and slipped through the kitchen door. She cautiously looked towards the entrance hall beyond.

Übung 85: Finden Sie ein passendes Synonym für die Wörter in Klammern!

"Be careful you don't (1. run into) ______________ the butler, Elvira!" whispered Hudson.

"Don't worry. This isn't the first time I've done something like this," she whispered back.

The inspector (2. groaned softly) __________. He had feared that.

He (3. followed) ________________ Elvira into the (4. enormous) ________________ entrance hall. He had seen station halls which were smaller. The wood-panelled walls held family portraits; proud aristocratic faces looked down at the inspector. Nearly disapprovingly as if they disapproved of him and Elvira trespassing in their home.

Elvira carefully opened a heavy oak door and (5. peered) ______ __________ into the room behind it. She saw a huge library with very old books and maps.

The next door opened into a drawing-room.

At the further end of the room there was an elegant bar in wood and in the (6. centre) __________________ an expensive billiard table.

The inspector picked up some courage and opened the next door himself. He looked into a large living room furnished with old leather armchairs and a heavy, tasteful oak table. In the corner stood an oak cupboard which probably elegantly hid a television. Hudson was absolutely sure the television only transmitted the BBC, that is, if it was ever used.

But something puzzled him. The rooms they had inspected so far, were elegantly furnished, but something in particular was missing. Hudson followed Elvira up a wide staircase to the first floor.
"Elvira," he whispered, "be careful. Remember, when we arrived, there was a light burning on the first floor. Somebody else apart from the butler is still awake!"
Elvira nodded. "Thank you for the warning, James. I'll be careful."
When they came to the top of the stairs, they saw a long, dark corridor. A dull light shone through the gap under the last door. Without hesitating or taking any notice of Hudson shaking his head, Elvira went towards it. Hushed voices could be heard in the room.

Übung 86: Finden und übersetzen Sie das bekannte Sprichwort, das sich im Text versteckt hat!

! ÜBUNG 86

A man coughed. A second man spoke in an encouraging tone, but Hudson could not understand what was being said.
But he recognised the voice – he had already heard it before. Forgetting his caution, he bent over and looked through the keyhole, which, for an inspector from Scotland Yard, was disgraceful. But the end justifies the means.

"What can you see?" asked Elvira softly. But the inspector did not answer or turn away from the keyhole. He had to concentrate on what the two men were saying.
On a wide, untidy bed, lay a young-looking man in his thirties. It must have been the present Lord Winterbutton. His similarity with the portraits was unmistakable. The lord was talking to another man who sat next to the bed.
Hudson recognised the small round figure immediately.
It was Cobblepot, the Winterbuttons' lawyer.

Übung 87: Lesen Sie weiter und unterstreichen Sie die „phrasal verbs"!

Now that Hudson could read their lips, it was easier for him to make out what was being said. "Don't worry Lord Stephen," said Sir Cobblepot and patted the young man's hand.
Lord Stephen laughed gratefully.
"Thank you Arthur. I'm very grateful that you dropped in on the eve of my thirty-third birthday, the family's horror day."
The lord coughed, Cobblepot shook his head.
"But, Stephen. You can't really believe this nonsense about the mummy's curse. You simply have a touch of flu, which is no surprise with this weather. All the rest is a stupid coincidence. In a couple of days you'll be laughing about this, I promise you."
Lord Winterbutton shook his head.
"No, Arthur. I don't believe it's a coincidence. But I have taken certain precautions to calm down Tut-Enk-Ra. I hope the curse will have soon left my family for ever."
Cobblepot was taken aback by this remark. The inspector was also surprised. What did Lord Winterbutton mean?
"Anyway, Stephen," said Cobblepot taking a small glass bottle out of his pocket, "I've brought along a vitamin preparation.

A simple vegetable mixture. My family has had this mixture prepared with a special recipe for a hundred years. It did my grandfather and father a lot of good. You should take a spoonful before going to sleep."
Lord Winterbutton nodded gratefully.
"You are a true friend, Arthur. Thank you. I don't know what I would do without you."
Cobblepot replied, "Oh, nonsense, Stephen. The Cobblepots have

been your family's lawyers and estate administrators for over a 150 years. I have to go now Stephen. I'll come and visit you in the morning if you wish."

Lord Winterbutton raised himself from his pillows to shake Cobblepot's hand.

"That would be nice, Arthur. See you tomorrow - and could you please close the door after you? When I have a fever I'm very sensitive to any noise."

"Of course. Good night, Stephen."

The lawyer nodded at the young man and went towards the door. Inspector Hudson stood up quickly.

Übung 88: Formulieren Sie die Sätze im Passiv.

1. Somebody stole the mummy from the museum.

____

2. The police are conducting some forensic tests.

____

3. Hudson will have solved the case.

____

4. Winterbutton opened the tomb straight away.

____

5. The butler did not invite Elvira and Hudson.

____

____

"What's wrong?" asked Elvira.

"Shhh!" Hudson pulled her away from the door.

They tiptoed to a dark corner in the corridor and hid in the shadow of an old grandfather clock. Just in the nick of time … thought the inspector.

A few seconds later the door opened and Cobblepot came out. Even in the dim light Hudson could see the satisfied grin on the lawyer's penguin face.

Cobblepot waggled down the stairs to the entrance hall. And left the house.

"Who was that?" asked Elvira.

"Lord Winterbutton's lawyer," replied Hudson. "I met him today at the 'Egyptian Society'. A rather unpleasant fellow, but obviously a trusted friend of Lord Winterbutton."

Elvira frowned.

"And does he know anything about the mummy theft?"

Übung 89: Wie lauten die Sätze richtig?

1. tiredly Lord Winterbutton himself raised his from pillows

2. thief into the broke The house

3. Before he dropped going home her off

4. is Hudson forward to looking day off his

5. Hudson the always assigned was cases difficult

____

6. into house the and broke stole some They portraits

____

7. he about know Does anything the mummy theft?

____

8. Egyptian is culture really interesting The

____

Hudson thought about it and shook his head.
"I don't think so," he answered. "Lord Winterbutton said something very strange about having taken measures against the curse … and Cobblepot seemed surprised about the fact."
"Taken measures against the curse?" repeated Elvira.
"What did he mean by that?"
Hudson frowned.
"I'm not sure, dear, but I have a suspicion. Did you notice anything strange in our little 'house visit'?"
Elvira looked at Hudson puzzled.
"No, what do you mean, James?"
"Well, do you remember that Lord Winterbutton – whether or not he has anything to do with the theft – owns the largest collection of Tut-Enk-Ra's relics?"
"Yes?"
"Elvira, apart from the door-knocker in the shape of a sphinx, there isn't one Egyptian relic to be seen in the whole house. The question is: Where did Lord Winterbutton hide his collection – and why on earth did he hide it?"

ÜBUNG 90 !

Übung 90: Lesen Sie weiter und korrigieren Sie die Wörter in Klammern!

Inspector Hudson and Elvira (1. quick) ________________ crept through the dark entrance hall. Luckily even the butler seemed to be asleep at this late hour and they were able to look around undisturbed.

"What are we looking for exactly?" asked Elvira.

The inspector looked around. He could be on the wrong track, but it was worth a try. For some reason or another, Lord Winterbutton (2. keeped) ________________ his Egyptian collection out of sight. And to hide such a large collection there was only one possibility: (3. it must being stored) ________________ in a cellar. And Hudson was sure that the old country house had a large underground vault.

"Let's look for it, Elvira!"

Hudson pointed to a wooden door in the entrance hall. It was smaller and less imposing (4. as) ________________ the other decorated oak doors which led to the drawing room and the lounge. (5. Without to wait) ________________ for Elvira to answer, Hudson went to the cellar door. It was not locked. A narrow, steep staircase lead down into the darkness. Directly (6. next the door)

_______________ was a switch, but the inspector did not want to risk turning the light on. (7. Lucky) _______________ Elvira had the solution.

Übung 91: Ordnen Sie die Satzhälften richtig zu! Tragen Sie die passende Ziffer in das Kästchen ein!

1. Elvira gave up smoking	☐ a) for years.
2. Elvira didn't give up smoking	☐ b) when Hudson first met her.
3. Elvira hadn't given up smoking	☐ c) years ago.
4. Elvira had given up smoking	☐ d) until she was 30.
5. Elvira had been trying to give up smoking	☐ e) by the time she was thirty.
6. Hudson didn't wait	☐ f) since 6 o'clock.
7. Hudson had been waiting	☐ g) until Elvira arrived.
8. Hudson was waiting here	☐ h) when Elvira finally arrived.
9. Hudson had been waiting an hour	☐ i) for long.
10. Hudson waited	☐ j) a minute ago.

She rummaged in her handbag and took out a flashlight. She was apparently prepared for everything. The inspector wondered how long she had been planning this unlawful entry.

But it was too late now to get cold feet. Hudson switched on the electric torch which had a surprisingly strong light. Hudson and Elvira went carefully down the stairs.
The temperature dropped after only a few steps.
"Brrr, it's cold down here," complained Elvira.
The inspector nodded. And by the looks of it, the cellar had been dug directly into the rock beneath the house.

ÜBUNG 92

Übung 92: Bilden Sie einen Relativsatz aus den zwei Sätzen!

1. This is the detective book. I was telling you about it.
   This is the detective book (which) I was telling you about.
2. Elvira is a friend. Hudson can always rely on her.

   ____
3. That's the man. The police were looking for him.

   ____
4. That is the mummy. The investigator is looking for it.

   ____
5. Sir Reginald is the boss. Hudson listens to him.

   ____
6. This is a clue. Hudson looked for it carefully.

   ____
7. That's his friend. He is sitting next to him.

   ____

They finally reached the actual cellar. The ceiling consisted of semi-arches. Hudson directed the electric torchlight throughout the enormous room. In the corners there was old furniture which had been carefully covered with sheets to avoid the dust. Looking at the silhouettes one could make out: various chairs, tables and cupboards.

"Wow," exclaimed Elvira, as she lifted a sheet and saw an old chest of drawers. "I know some antique dealers who would sell their grandmothers for such old antiques."

"Perhaps," replied Hudson, "but we're looking for much older items. Come Elvira."

The torch's light fell on another door which wasn't locked either. Hudson and Elvira went into the room on the other side carefully.

"Not bad," said Elvira and nodded approvingly.

Wooden wine racks stretched from one end of the cellar to another. There were no other doors.

Übung 93: Setzen Sie folgende Wörter in die Lücken!
(taste, size, torch, horizontally, label, trespassing)

"There must be at least a thousand bottles here," said Hudson and picked one up carefully. The 1. ______________ informed him that it was over 50 years old and therefore worth a fortune.

"It's nearly a pity to drink it," said Elvira. "The lord has good 2. ______________, but this is still not what we are looking for. And I can't see any other door. It looks like your instinct has let you down this time."

ÜBUNG 93 !

The inspector looked at the wine racks. Indeed, there were no other doors except for the one they had come through.

But something was wrong. Usually the cellar had the same surface area as the ground plan of the house. Considering the enormous 3. ________ of the house, the cellar should have been a lot bigger.

"Shouldn't we go back up?" asked Elvira at the door.

Hudson shook his head.

"I would like to look around a little longer," he answered.

"For me, we could open a bottle of wine and make ourselves comfortable," said Elvira laughing.

James shook his head.

"That way we could be charged with 4. __________ and burglary."

He looked carefully at the wine racks. The bottles lay 5. ______ ________ on the racks on all four walls.

Suddenly, the inspector directed his 6. ________________ onto the narrow side of the wine-vault.

"What have you seen?" cried Elvira.
"I don't know Elvira. But, look here at the wine rack."
Hudson went towards the wooden rack and Elvira followed him cautiously. The rack in front of them held dozens of bottles.
"Look at this," said Hudson pointing at the bottles.
"Yes," said Elvira. "There are a great deal of bottles like all the other racks."

Übung 94: Welche Gegenteile gehören zusammen? Setzen Sie die richtige Ziffer ein!

ÜBUNG 94 !

1. upright	☐ cry
2. right	☐ backwards
3. forwards	☐ horizontal
4. laugh	☐ wide
5. approve	☐ tiny
6. huge	☐ carelessly
7. carefully	☐ gradual
8. steep	☐ wrong
9. narrow	☐ disapprove

Smiling, Hudson replied, "Not exactly, Elvira. These bottles are vertical. All the other bottles are in a horizontal position."
"You're right!" exclaimed Elvira.
Then she picked up a vertical bottle and read the wine label.
"Mmmm, a 1999 Bordeaux," she murmured. "Enjoyable, but nothing special. I sometimes use it to cook with."
"It doesn't have much to do with all these vintage wines. I wonder why Lord Winterbutton would store such an ordinary bottle of wine here, in a vertical position."

Übung 95: Setzen Sie die Verben in der passenden Form (aktiv oder passiv) ein!

ÜBUNG 95 !

The insurance agent (1. put) ________________ the bottle back and (2. hold) ____________ the torch while Hudson tackled the rack. He gripped one side of the rack and pulled it.

And immediately the rack (3. give) ________________ way. It (4. swing) ____________ open to one side like a door.

"There you (5. be) ____________," (6. say) ____________ Hudson triumphantly. "Just like I thought. Another hidden vault!"

Elvira directed the torchlight in the room behind the door.

Both she and the inspector (7. freeze) ____________ with horror.

"Oh my God!" cried Elvira.

All of a sudden Hudson thought he (8. catapult) ____________ into another world. The torchlight no longer illuminated the dusty wine racks and antique furniture, but lit up an incredible splendour.

Hudson (9. can) ________________ not believe his eyes. And hearing Elvira's surprised gasps, he concluded that she was also astounded. Instead of a wine cellar, they were faced by an Egyptian death chamber. The walls were inlaid with stone slabs which (10. decorate) ________________ with reliefs of Egyptian gods.

The floor was tiled with gold flagstones.

Two oversized falcon gods watched over both sides of the entrance. However, the real eye catcher of the chamber was an oblong pedestal decorated with precious stones on which a gold-plated sarcophagus reposed.

"Incredible!" was all Elvira could say, for once at loss for words.

"W-what on earth is this here, James?" she asked bewildered.

James too was incredulous. He had expected to find Lord Winterbutton's Egyptian collection, but not a private museum!
"I think this is an exact imitation of Tut-Enk-Ra's tomb. Constructed with the family's collection …"
"… and the relics stolen all over the world!"
Elvira pointed at a small statue of a sacred cat whose diamond eyes flashed sinisterly.
"This cat was in the list of stolen relics. And this necklace on the pedestal too."

Übung 96: Ergänzen Sie die Sätze mit dem passenden „question tag"!

1. "You'd love a cup of tea, James, *wouldn't you*?"
2. Elvira won't forget her list of suspects, ____________________?
3. Let's go and visit Lord Winterbutton, ____________________?
4. It's a bit too late, ____________________?
5. Mr Cobblepot doesn't like Hudson, ____________________?
6. Elvira should drive more carefully, ____________________?
7. Drive more slowly, ____________________?
8. I'm in trouble, ____________________?

Hudson directed the torchlight on the pedestal. Indeed, there was a necklace near an empty, open sarcophagus.
"That is the mummy's jewellery, if I'm not mistaken," he said. "The question is – where's the mummy, Elvira?"
But the insurance agent was no longer standing next to Hudson

because she had gone deeper into the chamber, to have a close look at the precious antiquities.

"Incredible," she said once again. "I don't have my list with me, but I'm sure all the stolen relics from Tut-Enk-Ra's tomb are in this room. My company will be very happy."

Hudson nodded and followed Elvira into the tomb. He was happy for her. Her company would save millions of pounds and she would probably get a generous percentage as a reward.

But his task was not over yet. The stolen mummy was nowhere to be seen.

But it could not be far away.

! ÜBUNG 97

*Übung 97: Setzen Sie die richtige Form von **will** oder **going to** in die Lücke ein!*

1. Miss Paddington says to Hudson: "I ________________ make myself a cup of tea. Do you want one?"
2. Hudson __________ write a report when he has solved the case.
3. Do you think Hudson ________________ find the thief?
4. Why don't you check if the stolen goods on your list have anything in common. And I ________________ deal with my list about the access cards.
5. Miss Paddington says to Hudson "If you don't eat more, you ________________ become skin and bones."
6. Hudson says "I (not) ________________ work today. I'm tired."

7. Hudson says "It's hot in this room" and Miss Paddington answers "I ________________ open the window."
8. Hudson asks Elvira "Where ________________ to spend your next holiday?"
9. There are some very black clouds in the sky. It ________ ________ rain again.

Inspector Hudson took a step forward and nearly tripped over an uneven flagstone. He looked down. The golden tiles covering the floor were decorated with reliefs portraying various Egyptian gods, some of whom Hudson knew:
the sun god Horus with his falcon head, Bastet the cat goddess and the fertility god Osiris.

Übung 98: Welches Wort ist das „schwarze Schaf"?

ÜBUNG 98 !

1. onwards, forwards, towards, on ________________
2. always, often, between, sometimes ________________
3. have, would, should, must ________________
4. heavy, weight, scale, width ________________
5. death, after-life, depth, eternal repose ________________
6. surprised, astounded, shocked, alive ________________
7. trespass, break in, run away, burgle ________________
8. suspect, criminal, offender, policeman ________________

And Elvira herself stepped towards a tile depicting Anubis, the death god with a jackal head.
"Elvira!" cried Hudson. "Don't move!"
Elvira looked at him surprised. Her foot was suspended over the gold tile with Anubis.
"I've just thought of something," he said. "If this is a 1:1 reconstruction of the real chamber, then Lord Winterbutton might have also copied the deathtrap which was in the original tomb."
"Deathtrap?" gasped Elvira and looked down at the jackal-headed god at her feet.
"What an unpleasant god," she said.
"Not necessarily," explained Hudson. "Anubis only checked who deserved to be redeemed and who was to be sent to the underworld. And considering your dissipated lifestyle, I wouldn't step on it if I were you."
"Very funny, James," retorted Elvira. "But do you really believe that this flagstone will trigger a deathtrap?"

! ÜBUNG 99

*Übung 99: Schreiben Sie einen passenden Satz mit den Wörtern in Klammern! Nutzen Sie **might**, **must** oder **could**!*

1. Lord Winterbutton has got a cough. (might, bronchitis)

   He might have bronchitis.

2. He looks very miserable. (must, afraid, die)

   ____

3. He doesn't have any Egyptian relics in his house. (might, hide)

   ____

4. Hudson has been working all day. (must, deadline to meet)

____

5. Why are there two lights on in Lord Winterbutton's house? (could, be awake)

____

6. I wonder how the thief got into the museum? (must, use access card)

____

7. It's nearly midnight. (Lord Winterbutton, might, sleep)

____

8. All the Winterbuttons died on their thirty-third birthday. (must, be unlucky)

____

9. How did the burglar get into our apartment? (he could, use, fire escape)

____

The inspector kneeled down carefully next to the golden tile on the floor. In the torchlight it was easy to see that the grooves of the tile were wider than the bordering tiles.
"I'm nearly sure ...," he answered thoughtfully. "It is likely that there is a spring mechanism beneath it, which is linked to a trap.

The ancient Egyptians knew how to protect their graves."
Suddenly a ceiling light was turned on. The light reflected itself a thousand times on the golden relics in the death chamber.

ÜBUNG 100

Übung 100: Ordnen Sie die Buchstaben zu einem sinnvollen Wort!

"Luckily my great-grandfather knew all the (1. rictks) ________!" cried a voice.

Inspector Hudson blinked in the dazzling light. He could just make out two figures standing at the entrance of the (2. mbot) ________. His eyes slowly became accustomed to the light and he recognised Winterbutton and his wide-shouldered (3. reltub) ________. Winterbutton looked even paler than he did in bed. He had to lean on the butler's shoulder. However, he still looked angrily at the two trespassers.

"May I ask with whom I have the unexpected pleasure?" asked the lord. Hudson assumed an official attitude and tried to inspire (4. uathroyit) ________________, which was a little difficult considering he had been (5. ghtcau) ________________ trespassing.

"I'm (6. rotcepsin) ________ James Hudson from Scotland Yard," he said and pointed to Elvira. "And my assistant Miss Elliot."

"Assistant, did I hear correctly?" whispered Elvira and gave him a little push.
"Not now, Elvira," whispered Hudson back and turned his attention to Lord Winterbutton.
"Please excuse our unconventional admission, but we suspected that you had something to do with the disappearance of the mummy, Lord Winterbutton."

Übung 101: Unterstreichen Sie die direkte Rede!

ÜBUNG 101 !

"With the disappearance of the mummy!" said Elvira angrily. "You mean with the theft of the Egyptian mummy, just like all the other thefts. Half the relics have been stolen from all around the world."
Lord Winterbutton sighed and looked guiltily at the floor.
"I'm afraid you're right, sir. But I had my good reasons."
Inspector Hudson shook his head. The young lord looked a picture of misery, but he was after all guilty of several thefts. And he had just confessed.
"And I have good reasons to arrest you, Lord Winterbutton!" said Hudson sternly. But Lord Winterbutton shook his head looking sadly.
"I'm very sorry, but I can't allow that. It would be my death sentence."

Then he nodded at his butler. Without hesitating the butler rushed forward. With three limping, but quick steps he reached the inspector and the insurance agent.
But he wasn't prepared for Elvira's belligerence. She suddenly pushed the surprised inspector aside and stood in the butler's way. The wide-shouldered man wanted to thrash Elvira, but she dodged

him and grabbed his wrist and whirled him over her shoulder onto the floor. The man hit the golden-tiled floor with a bang and lay there moaning.

Both Hudson and Lord Winterbutton had watched the scene with their mouths gaping. Elvira looked from one to another.

"And that'll be that!" she said.

Inspector Hudson swallowed. He was really glad Elvira was on his side.

"I'm sorry Lord Winterbutton, but I have to arrest you now. And your employee for attacking an officer on duty."

Lord Winterbutton became even paler. He took a few steps forward, then he had to hold onto the empty sarcophagus to avoid falling down.

! ÜBUNG 102

*Übung 102: Übersetzen Sie die Verben ins Englische! Wann kommt **oneself** hinzu?*

1. sich ändern ________________
2. sich verletzen ________________
3. sich fühlen ________________
4. sich erinnern ________________
5. sich amüsieren ________________
6. auf sich achten ________________

"No, inspector, you can't arrest me. It would be like killing me!" he cried. Inspector Hudson frowned.

“You said something like that before!” he said. “What do you mean?”
Hudson felt really sorry for the young man. Elvira, too, took a step forward to stop the aristocrat from falling.
The lord sighed.

Übung 103: Setzen Sie die richtige Präposition in die Lücke!

1. Are you afraid _______________ the dark cellar?
2. Who is responsible _______________ cleaning the museum?
3. London is famous _______________ the rain.
4. Lord Winterbutton should be ashamed _________ what he did.
5. What’s wrong _______________ Lord Winterbutton? He looks a little pale.
6. Elvira is excited _______________ finding the thief.
7. Hudson is not used _______________ relaxing in the morning.
8. Lord Winterbutton is grateful _______________ Hudson’s help.
9. Miss Paddington’s reaction _________ the news was surprise.
10. She was very shocked _______________ the news.
11. Hudson was suspicious _______________ the butler.
12. Elvira is very good _______________ her job.

“The curse of the mummy, inspector. Tut-Enk-Ra put a curse on my whole family because my great-grandfather disturbed his eternal repose. And that is why I brought everything here. The Pharaoh's whole death chamber. Some of the relics here are a part of the family collection. My faithful butler stole the rest."

The lord pointed to his butler who still lay dazed on the floor.

"I'm ashamed of what I have done – but I had no other choice. My thirty-third birthday is just around the corner, and you can already see that I am unwell."

Suddenly the inspector understood what Lord Winterbutton had in mind.

"My God, Lord Winterbutton," he exclaimed, "you built an exact imitation of the death chamber in your cellar …"

"… so that the Pharaoh could have his peace back and take back the curse!" finished Elvira.

Winterbutton nodded.

ÜBUNG 104 !

Übung 104: Finden Sie die Nomen zu den Verben!

1. discuss ______________________
2. suspect ______________________
3. advise ______________________
4. exclaim ______________________
5. enquire ______________________
6. imitate ______________________
7. employ ______________________

"I'm very sorry I involved my butler in the thefts, but I could see no other way. Once I had all the treasures together again, the mummy was the only missing piece. I lent George, my butler, the access card to the British Museum and prepared the death chamber here in my cellar. Tonight I was going to put the prince back in his tomb and seal this room forever. But a while ago, after my lawyer had left, I heard your voices in the corridor. Because of the fever, my ears are very sensitive to noises."

Hudson nodded. He and Elvira had been very careless. Luckily the whole episode had ended without much harm being done.

"Lord Winterbutton," he said in a soothing tone, "I can assure you that the mummy's curse is just superstition. You are in no danger."

"I wouldn't be so sure of that," said a voice behind them.

Inspector Hudson turned around.

None of them had heard Arthur Cobblepot arrive.

The small fat man still reminded the inspector of a penguin. A penguin holding a pistol.

Übung 105: Übersetzen Sie die Wörter in Klammern!

ÜBUNG 105 !

"Arthur!" exclaimed Lord Winterbutton, shocked. "What are you doing? Why are you holding a gun?"

Cobblepot (1. grinste) ____________________.

"Well, dear Stephen, because you were a naughty boy and didn't take your medicine, I'm forced to take drastic (2. Mittel) ____________________."

"M-My medicine?" he (3. fragte) ____________________, "I don't understand."

"I do!" exclaimed Hudson. "The so-called tonic is (4. Gift) ________________, isn't it, Cobblepot? How long have you been giving it to Lord Winterbutton?"

"Oh, for quite some time, inspector," answered the (5. Rechtsanwalt) ________________. "However, I was only following a family tradition." Cobblepot cackled.

Hudson took a deep breath. Now he understood what a horrible (6. Verbrechen) ________________ he and Elvira had come across. Only Lord Winterbutton did not seem to understand. Perhaps the shock was too much for him.

"What do you mean, Arthur?" he asked.

Cobblepot cackled again.

"Oh Stephen, you Winterbuttons have never been very (7. schlau) ________________. That's why my family had so little trouble gaining your (8. Vertrauen) ____________."

"Good Arthur Cobblepot tried to poison you, Stephen," interrupted Hudson, "just like his father poisoned your father, and his grandfather poisoned your grandfather. Not so Cobblepot?"
"Certainly," replied the lawyer proudly and waved his gun around. "As I said, it was a family tradition."
Lord Winterbutton went even paler. His world was going to pieces. "But why, Cobblepot?"
"It's very simple, dear Stephen – to profit from your family. Every

Übung 106: Unterstreichen Sie das richtige Modalverb!

1. You shouldn't/mustn't have any problem with the surveillance system.
2. You don't have to/mustn't wear wellingtons in the rain, but they keep your feet drier.
3. Hudson couldn't/wouldn't have a relaxing day off because Sir Reginald called him for a case.
4. Elvira's so stubborn. She can't/won't do what she is told.
5. Hudson was able to/could obtain a copy of the surveillance tape.
6. "You don't have to/mustn't say a word about working with me," said Hudson to Elvira.
7. Hudson should have obtained/had to obtain a search warrant to enter Lord Winterbutton's home, but Elvira was too impatient.

time a Winterbutton died, my family took care of the inheritance and we kept a lot of the family's fortune. Two hundred thousand pounds here, a little property there – you have no idea, Stephen, how rich your family would be if we hadn't been your lawyers for such a long time."

"And the curse of the mummy?" asked Elvira.

She was also very shocked at the young lawyer's cold-bloodedness.

"All nonsense," replied Cobblepot. "After opening the tomb, the old Douglas Winterbutton died of a normal tropical fever. My grandfather took advantage of the legend to poison your grandfather thirty-three years later. Just like my father poisoned your father on his thirty-third birthday. And now it was my turn to get rid of you, Stephen, if only you hadn't had this foolish idea of stealing the mummy to put the curse to an end."

Übung 107: Welche Präposition muss in die Lücke?

1. daran denken	think *of*
2. unfähig sein zu …	be incapable ___
3. in der Angst leben, dass …	live in fear ___
4. glauben an …	believe ___
5. darauf bestehen, dass …	insist ___
6. schwierig finden zu …	have difficulty ___
7. sich interessieren für …	be interested ___
8. davon träumen zu …	dream ___

Cobblepot cackled again and pointed the gun at the lord.
"Well, I'll close you and the two nosy-parkers in this chamber. And nobody will ever see you again. Actually it'll be even better if you disappear without a trace, because as your estate administrator I'll have free disposition of your fortune."
However, when Cobblepot released the gun's safety catch, Hudson had had enough. He slowly walked towards the fraudulent lawyer. "That's enough Cobblepot," he said sternly. "You can't get away with this. Put down the gun."
Cobblepot pointed his gun at Hudson
"Don't come any closer," he threatened. "Or I'll pull the trigger!"

Übung 108: Verbinden Sie die zwei passenden Satzteile und setzen Sie die richtige Ziffer in das Kästchen!

1. I'm ashamed
2. Inspector Hudson
3. The main entrance
4. He seemed rather excited

5. The sports car
6. All the equipment
7. When they came

- [ ] at the idea of helping Scotland Yard in an investigation.
- [ ] of what I have done.
- [ ] was driven by either a madman or a reporter.
- [ ] to the top of the stairs, they saw a long, dark corridor.
- [ ] was surrounded by a large crowd of photographers.
- [ ] had to be transported on camels.
- [ ] took a step forward.

Hudson took a deep breath and took another step. Instinctively Cobblepot stepped backwards and aimed at Hudson's head.
"James!" screamed Elvira. "He'll shoot you!"
"Listen to your friend!" said Cobblepot while Hudson took yet another step forward.
Cobblepot took a step backwards. Then he screamed.
A gun shot rang through the tomb.

Übung 109: Beantworten Sie die folgenden Fragen zum Text!

ÜBUNG 109 !

1. What did Hudson and Elvira find exactly?

____

2. What was missing in the death chamber?

____

3. What happened to the butler?

____

4. Why did the Cobblepots poison one Winterbutton after another?

____

5. What did Cobblepot want to do to Elvira and Hudson?

____

Inspector Hudson's plan had worked. He had imagined that Cobblepot would step backwards before pulling the trigger.
And so the killer lawyer stepped on the flagstone with the engraving of Anubis the death god.
And as the inspector had expected, the flagstone set off the trap. The flagstone gave way and Cobblepot fell into a hole. He instinctively pulled the trigger as he was falling, but the bullet flew harmlessly over Hudson's head.
Hudson, Elvira and Lord Winterbutton all ran to the edge of the narrow hole. The little fat man was wedged in the narrow, two metre deep hole. Unhurt but wailing.
"Get me out of here!" he cried. "I'm stuck."
Anger had given Lord Winterbutton's cheeks a bit of colour.
"You horrible man. You're lucky that I didn't make a real death trap. In the real tomb the hole was full of snakes.

ÜBUNG 110 !

Übung 110: Setzen Sie die richtige Verbform ein!

The inspector couldn't help smiling.

"Tell us if there is an antidote against the poison you (1. give) ____________________ poor Lord Winterbutton. Then we (2. pull) ________________ you out of the deathtrap."

Cobblepot shook his head in a panic.

"Lord Winterbutton (3. not need) ______________ an antidote. His body (4. eliminate) ______________ the poison on its own. I wanted to give the fatal dose tonight."

Lord Winterbutton sighed in relief. The prospect of (5. be) ______________ rid of the curse made him feel better already.

"Thank God," he coughed.

In that moment they (6. hear) ______________ the chimes of the grandfather clock in the corridor. It was midnight.

Lord Winterbutton (7. overjoy) ______________.

"12 o'clock. Today is my birthday. My thirty-third birthday!"

Hudson patted the young aristocrat on the shoulder.

"And you also (8. celebrate) ______________ your thirty-fourth birthday, Lord Winterbutton!" he said.

Elvira (9. go) ______________ up to the lord and gave him a kiss on the forehead.

"Happy birthday, dearie!" she said.

Inspector Hudson gratefully took the cup of steaming tea from the tray that Miss Paddington was holding.
Then he took a sip of the Earl Grey and leaned back in his armchair. It was nine o'clock in the morning and outside it was drizzling.

Übung 111: Übersetzen Sie die folgenden Sätze!

1. Elvira Elliot hatte ein halb geöffnetes Fenster gefunden und drückte es vorsichtig auf.

2. Langsam gewöhnten sich seine Augen an die Dunkelheit.

3. Er freute sich für die Versicherungsagentin, da ihre Auftraggeber Millionen von Pfund sparen würden.

4. Hudson traute seinen Augen nicht, denn was vor ihnen lag, war kein Keller, sondern eine ägyptische Totenkammer.

5. Zum Glück schien auch der Butler zu dieser späten Stunde bereits zu schlafen.

6. Es brannte Licht in einem der Stockwerke, so waren beide vorsichtig.

7. Trotz der späten Stunde dauerte es nur ein paar Sekunden, bis ein Mann in einer Butleruniform die Tür öffnete.

____

____

"And what will happen to Lord Winterbutton?" asked Miss Paddington nearly worried.
Hudson had got home very late. First they had pulled the trembling Sir Cobblepot out of the hole. Then Hudson had informed the police and had had to fill in several forms.
And lastly Elvira had insisted that they celebrate the day in one of those downtown cocktail bars in London.
And although the inspector had arrived home in the middle of the night, absolutely exhausted, Miss Paddington had obliged him to tell her the whole story of the case.
But at least he could catch up on his day off today.

Übung 112: Geben Sie die richtige Präposition nach dem Verb an!

ÜBUNG 112 !

1. They accused him ______ stealing the mummy from the museum.
2. Hudson prevented Lord Winterbutton ______________ being poisoned by Sir Cobblepot.
3. Hudson warned Elvira ____________ trespassing.
4. Lord Winterbutton apologised ____________ stealing the relics.
5. Hudson succeeded ____________ solving the case in 24 hours.
6. Elvira thanked Hudson ___________ letting her work with him.

Hudson took another sip of tea and looked at the housekeeper.
"Well, he did after all involve his butler in numerous thefts. But it was in a way in self defence. I think both will get off with a short suspended sentence. Anyhow, both are very happy that the whole nightmare is over. The Winterbuttons have had to live long enough with the fear of the 'curse'."
"So the curse of the mummy was just hocus-pocus?" asked Miss Paddington.
Mr Hudson shook his head slowly.
"Well, no matter what people thought it was, two members of the Winterbutton family lost their lives because of the tomb desecration. So in a certain way, the curse did come true. And Stephen Winterbutton was the first one who wanted to give back the mummy its peace – and this had also saved his life. The British Museum has agreed to let the mummy be taken back to Egypt together with the relics owned by the Winterbutton family."

ÜBUNG 113 !

Übung 113: Geben Sie die richtigen Formen von ***to steal*** *an!*

1. einfache Gegenwart: *he steals*
2. Verlaufsform der Gegenwart: ______________
3. Einfache Vergangenheit: ______________
4. Vergangenheit mit "used to": ______________
5. Verlaufsform der Vergangenheit: ______________
6. present perfect: ______________
7. Verlaufsform des present perfect: *he has been stealing*

8. Plusquamperfekt: ____________

9. Verlaufsform des Plusquamperfekts: ____________

10. Zukunft mit "going to": ____________

11. Zukunft mit "will": ____________

12. future perfect: *he will have stolen*

13. Verlaufsform des future perfect: ____________

Miss Paddington thought about it for a few seconds and then, once again, turned her attention to practical things.

"I'll prepare you something for breakfast, James," she said in a motherly tone. "You look hungry. Lean back and enjoy your day off at last."

Then she went with determined steps towards the kitchen.

Inspector closed his eyes and sighed.

Outside the rain pattered on the window. In the kitchen Miss Paddington's pots and pans banged. There was the usual thump outside the door when the newspaper was delivered.

Hudson did not even get a fright when the phone rang.

A few seconds later, Miss Paddington entered the room.

"It's for you, Sir Reginald is on the phone. It's about some magician who disappeared during a performance yesterday and hasn't turned up since. Sir Reginald thinks it's the right case for you."

Hudson opened his eyes and took another sip of tea.

"Tell him I'm on my way," he sighed.

THE END

Abschlusstest

Übung 1: Unterstreichen Sie die richtige Form des Präsens!

1. Hudson drinks/is drinking tea at the moment.
2. What is he doing/does he do today?
3. Elvira usually travels/is travelling by plane to Europe.
4. Hudson always knows/is knowing what to do.
5. He is looking/looks for clues.
6. It rains/is raining outside.

Übung 2: Schreiben Sie die Sätze im „first conditional“!

1. If the phone had not rung Inspector Hudson (enjoy) his day off.

   ____

2. Elvira (like) to work on the case with Hudson.

   ____

3. Sir Reginald (not put) anyone else in charge of the case.

   ____

*Übung 3: Verbinden Sie das **phrasal verb** mit der richtigen englischen Erklärung! Setzen Sie die Ziffer ein!*

1. to find out	☐	a) admit responsibility
2. to turn up	☐	b) not stay at home
3. to own up	☐	c) arrive uninvited
4. to go out	☐	d) wait
5. to hold on	☐	e) meet/find by chance
6. to come across	☐	f) discover

Übung 4: Schreiben Sie Datum und Uhrzeit aus!

1. 7. Januar 2003 ____________________________
2. 18.45 Uhr ____________________________
3. Morgen um 12.00 mittags ____________________________
4. Am fünften Mai ____________________________
5. Zehn Minuten vor sechs, heute Abend ______________
____
6. 1812 ____________________________

Übung 5: Welche Präpositionen passen?

1. ________ Christmas
2. ________ the world
3. ________ the beach
4. ________ the end
5. ________ a concert
6. ________ the phone
7. ________ the morning
8. ________ summer
9. ________ night

Übung 6: ***Some*** *oder* ***any, much*** *oder* ***many*** *oder* ***a lot of****?*

1. Hudson has brought ____________ friends to the Yard.
2. Elvira never gets ____________ information about James.
3. Is there ____________ tea left?
4. He hasn't got ____________ time?
5. Hudson did have ____________ trouble.
6. Elvira thinks she knows ____________ history.
7. Miss Paddington has got ____________ nice ideas.

Lösungen

Übung 1: sighed, closed, listened, tried, grinned, continued, suggested
Übung 2: 1. smiled 2. waited 3. rained 4. did not 5. grumbled 6. went 7. was 8. thought 9. frowned 10. entered 11. laughed 12. answered 13. replied
Übung 3: 1. walk 2. yesterday 3. house 4. search 5. book 6. man 7. dry 8. noise
Übung 4: 1. He lives in a flat in London. 2. Miss Paddington is Hudson's housekeeper. 3. He hears the clock ticking, a crashing sound, the rain, the thump of a newspaper, the squeaking of a bicycle and Miss Paddington's curses. 4. He has tea, toast and marmalade for breakfast. 5. He reads The London Times.
Übung 5: did/do, rang/ring, let/let, had/have, was/be, let/let, thought/think, said/say, knew/know, could/can
Übung 6: 1. clue 2. robbery 3. find out 4. murder 5. police Lösung: crime
Übung 7: 1. a, the 2. a 3. An, a 4. a 5. an 6. – 7. the, a 8. The
Übung 8: 1. newspapers 2. thieves 3. women 4. men 5. potatoes 6. mice 7. knives 8. oxen 9. foxes 10. lobbies
Übung 9: 1. Where does Mr Hudson live? 2. How does he go to work? 3. Whose car is that? 4. What sort of car is it? 5. How often does Mr Hudson read the newspaper? 6. When does the museum close? 7. Who is Miss Paddington? 8. What's this book about? 9. How much does it cost? 10. When did he close his last case? 11. Why does Mr Hudson like his car so much?
Übung 10: 1. building 2. entrance 3. rain 4. museum 5. stopped 6. smell 7. discover
Übung 11: 1. display/exhibit 2. see/look 3. find out/discover 4. make/do 5. help/assist 6. investigate/gather evidence 7. arrest/catch 8. escape/run away 9. steal/rob
Übung 12: 1. caught 2. stole 3. knew 4. shook 5. brought 6. saw 7. came 8. went 9. began 10. won 11. slept 12. took 13. could 14. ate 15. had
Übung 13: constable, room, way, site, crime, pieces, childhood, empire, years, findings, relics
Übung 14: 1. I'm not 2. We aren't 3. He wasn't 4. I won't 5. I didn't 6. She can't 7. He didn't steal 8. You haven't stolen 9. I haven't got 10. He doesn't steal 11. you don't dream
Übung 15: 1. criminal 2. brusque 3. surprised 4. scene 5. grin 6. recalled 7. enquired
Übung 16: 1. lost/lost 2. ring/rung 3. think/thought 4. woke/woken 5. speak/spoken 6. steal/stole 7. shot/shot 8. sit/sat 9. paid/paid 10. hit/hit 11. taught/taught
Übung 17: 1. falsch 2. falsch 3. richtig 4. falsch 5. richtig 6. falsch 7. falsch
Übung 18: 1. an 2. a 3. some 4. a 5. a 6. some 7. an 8. some 9. an 10. some 11. some
Übung 19: 1. reply/ask 2. rainy/dry 3. speak/listen 4. yes/no 5. finish/start 6. sad/happy 7. cold/hot 8. panic/calm 9. sick/healthy
Übung 20: 1. by 2. on 3. at 4. of 5. on 6. with 7. in

Übung 21: 1. Inspector Hudson loved the soft noises. 2. James let the phone ring twice. 3. He read the first page again. 4. A minute later Miss Paddington came into the living room. 5. The constable looked at him confused. 6. Perhaps the mummy had an accomplice. 7. Hudson concentrated on the screen.
Übung 22: 1. any 2. some, any 3. any 4. any 5. some 6. some 7. any
Übung 23: 1. Do you often go to the museum? 2. I never drink tea because I don't like it. 3. Hudson is never late for work. 4. My housekeeper always watches the news in the evening. 5. The inspector rarely has a day off. 6. The old car braked suddenly. 7. The cars hooted at the pedestrians loudly.
Übung 24: violently, similarly, always, obviously, well, proudly, snobbishly
Übung 25: 1. at 2. on 3. at 4. in 5. in 6. at 7. at 8. at 9. on 10. in 11. in 12. at
Übung 26: 1. gut, gesund 2. ziemlich, hübsch 3. nur, einzig 4. gerade, gerecht
Übung 27: 1. caught 2. known 3. shaken 4. brought 5. seen 6. come 7. gone 8. begun 9. won 10. slept 11. taken 12. could
Übung 28: 1. works 2. It's raining 3. lives 4. is drinking 5. is looking 6. brings 7. thinks
Übung 29: 1. drizzling 2. meeting 3. impatiently 4. parties 5. throat 6. tip 7. over
Übung 30: 1. c 2. b 3. c 4. c 5. a 6. b
Übung 31: 1. He would never admit that he liked Elvira. 2. The motive would give Hudson a clue about the thief. 3. Inspector Hudson would be proud of her. 4. He would find out who had stolen the mummy. 5. It was more money that he would ever earn at the Yard. 6. He would work together with her. 7. But Sir Reginald would never find out.
Übung 32: 1. happier/happiest 2. better/best 3. younger/youngest 4. more/most beautiful 5. worse/worst 6. more/most comfortable 7. busier/busiest 8. more/most patient 9. more/most polite 10. further/furthest
Übung 33: 1. anything 2. Nobody 3. Nothing, anything 4. anywhere 5. Nobody, anything 6. nobody 7. anything
Übung 34: Well, what should he do, thought Hudson. – After all, if it hadn't been for Elvira, he might never have known about the other thefts. – It was only fair to let her take part in the investigation. – Sir Reginald must never know of it, though. – Hopefully he would not regret this decision.
Übung 35: 1. straight/crooked 2. back/front 3. wealthy/poor 4. young/elderly 5. freezing/boiling 6. hard-working/lazy 7. laugh/cry 8. outgoing/reserved 9. black/white 10. grow/decrease 11. tumult/calm 12. devil/angel 13. broken/intact 14. diverse/identical 15. seldom/often
Übung 36: 1. defence 2. charge 3. manslaughter 4. sentence 5. stole 6. killed 7. guilty
Übung 37: had not answered the phone, had been sitting, had laid down, had been busy, had not come across, had cheated, had not led, had been stolen

Übung 38: 1. holiday 2. evidence 3. proof 4. the city 5. church 6. a member 7. good old Elvira
Übung 39: 1. Because he wanted Hudson to answer the reporters' questions at the press conference. 2. She was searching for information on the stolen relics. 3. Because he's old-fashioned. In fact he also has an old car.
Übung 40: 1. a swarm of bees 2. a pack of wolves 3. a flight of birds 4. a herd of cattle 5. a pack of hyenas 6. a school of fish 7. a gaggle of geese
Übung 41: 1. pulled 2. sat 3. could 4. was 5. was doing 6. came across 7. took 8. have been stolen
Übung 42: 1. A Bentley is more expensive than a Ford. 2. A clock is bigger than a watch. 3. A pyramid is higher than a sphinx. 4. A town is larger than a village. 5. A lake is deeper than a pond. 6. A tree is taller than a bush. 7. Germany is bigger than England.
Übung 43: 1. broke into 2. came across 3. find out 4. was after 5. looking for 6. take good care of 7. give up
Übung 44: 1. twenty-six 2. second 3. first 4. thirtieth 5. half 6. nineteen thirty-three 7. eight hundred and fifty-three thousand 8. five point seven eight 9. three-quarters
Übung 45: murmured, said, exclaimed, cried, asked
Übung 46: 1. still 2. yet 3. still 4. any more/any longer 5. no longer 6. still
Übung 47: 1. fill in a form 2. put away clothes in a cupboard 3. sort out a problem 4. find out information 5. try on clothes in a shop 6. try out a new idea 7. bring up children 8. take back something you don't want 9. put off a meeting 10. clear up a mess 11. put out a fire
Übung 48: 1. grinned 2. has/possesses 3. relics 4. grave 5. nobleman 6. chance/fluke 7. breathed out
Übung 49: 1. which/that 2. where 3. which 4. who 5. whose 6. which oder nichts 7. when oder nichts 8. which/that
Übung 50: 1. richtig 2. richtig 3. falsch 4. richtig 5. falsch 6. richtig 7. richtig
Übung 51: 1. have announced 2. were stolen 3. were valued 4. were taken 5. did not go off 6. was not discovered 7. have been found
Übung 52: 1. c 2. b 3. a 4. b 5. b 6. c 7. b
Übung 53: "Good afternoon, old chap," he called, "where can I park my car, please?" – "I'm sorry sir, the club and its parking places are for members only."
"Arrogant pig!" whispered Elvira from the passenger seat. – "I don't have a member's card, but perhaps this will open the door to your respectable rooms." – "Scotland Yard? I'm very sorry, sir. I didn't know. You may park directly behind the building in the guests' parking place." – "Now, Elvira," said Hudson regretfully, "I'm afraid the authority of my badge is not enough to get you into the club as well."
Übung 54: James asked where he could park his car. 2. James said he did not have

a member's card. 3. James said that perhaps his badge would let him in. 4. The porter said he could park behind the building. 5. Elvira said she would read the diary. 6. Miss Paddington said that he had promised to rest. 7. Elvira asked James what he was looking for.

Übung 55: 1. clue 2. red herring 3. alibi 4. witness 5. inspector 6. Evidence 7. Suspects

Übung 56: 1. give up/surrender 2. imagination/fantasy 3. spirits/morale 4. trace/hint 5. picked up/caught 6. perplexed/puzzled 7. medication/drugs 8. sceptics/doubters

Übung 57: 1. gone 2. been 3. been 4. been 5. gone 6. been 7. gone

Übung 58: 2. Hudson sits in his bureau listening to the radio. 3. Elvira finds out a lot reading the books. 4. Miss Paddington came into the kitchen wanting to cook for dinner. 5. The man walks away looking a little pale.

Übung 59: from ... to, around, next to, in, through

Übung 60: 1. wasted 2. well-off 3. will 4. safe 5. salary 6. coin 7. broke

Übung 61: 1. perfectly 2. carefully 3. heavily 4. well 5. fast 6. hard 7. late

Übung 62: 1. something 2. hurry up 3. best 4. direct 5. nice 6. rarely 7. real 8. outside 9. agreement 10. raised

Übung 63: 1. hardly 2. hard 3. Hardly 4. well 5. good 6. lately 7. late

Übung 64: 1. In the meantime, Hudson had had time to brew some tea and serve Elvira a cup. 2. In 1903 Lord Douglas Winterbutton discovered Tut-Enk-Ra's tomb by chance. 3. It rang at least a dozen times before someone picked up the phone at the other end. 4. Inspector Hudson said goodbye and got out the car. 5. A couple of the guests turned around surprised. 6. Mr Cornwall pointed to two free armchairs which were next to each other in the corner of the room. 7. Patience was definitely not a virtue Elvira possessed.

Übung 65: began, started, was, was heading, aimed at, knew, had existed, was, thought, was, would obtain, squander, regarded, was married, was expecting, was, took, was, had to be transported, were, help, find

Übung 66: 1. hunger 2. friend 3. dizzy 4. widow 5. penguin 6. dish 7. author

Übung 67: 1. falsch 2. falsch 3. richtig 4. falsch 5. richtig 6. falsch 7. richtig

Übung 68: 2. would not be/ate 3. didn't have to work/could meet 4. would taste/had 5. would know/had 6. were/would live 7. would buy/earned 8. listened/would make

Übung 69: 1. bigger, biggest 2. more nervous, most nervous 3. thirstier, thirstiest 4. politer, politest 5. more, most 6. better, best 7. quieter, quietest 8. further, furthest 9. luckier, luckiest 10. more careful, most careful

Übung 70: 2. he were/was here 3. I didn't live there 4. he had a new one 5. he were/was younger 6. he were/was thinner and taller 7. knew

Übung 71: 1. angry 2. beam 3. boiling 4. exhausted 5. shout 6. terrified 7. argue

Übung 72: thin/skin and bones, smiling/beaming, appreciatively/gratefully, lounge/living room, start again/resume, presently/before long, hollow/empty

Übung 73: 1. driving licence 2. steering wheel 3. insurance agent 4. airport 5. birthday card 6. motorway 7. country estate 8. sun glasses 9. headlights
Übung 74: 1. He had to go abroad quite often. 2. The Winterbutton family had been unlucky. 3. The thief must have done it. 4. Hudson may not /is not allowed to drink on duty.
Übung 75: Adverbien: carefully, slowly, gruffly, luckily, probably, really, curiously
Adjektive: fast, sporty, unsporty, slower, safe, sound, wrong, moderate
Übung 76: 1. wouldn't have answered 2. hadn't driven/wouldn't have got 3. had given/wouldn't have gone 4. had been/wouldn't have gone 5. hadn't followed/wouldn't have found out 6. hadn't gone/wouldn't have died
Übung 77: 1. ruin 2. prince 3. violence 4. estate 5. suspect 6. tomb 7. coincidence 8. interrogate 9. paperboy 10. descendant 11. die 12. tongue 13. pain
Lösung: investigation
Übung 78: 1. much 2. Many 3. a lot of 4. Many 5. much 6. many 7. a lot 8. a lot of 9. a lot
Übung 79: 1. unless 2. before 3. But 4. too 5. Only
Übung 80: 1. he goes 2. he is going 3. he went 4. he used to go 5. he was going 6. he has gone 7. he has been going 8. he had gone 9. he had been going 10. he is going to go 11. he will go 12 he will have gone 13. he will have been going
Übung 81: 1. ancient/old 2. automobile/car 3. dead/deceased 4. enquire/ask 5. cop/policeman 6. steal/pinch 7. strange/bizzare 8. drink/sip
Übung 82: 1. wasn't listening 2. was staring 3. had rung 4. is 5. took 6. was trying 7. came
Übung 83: 1. His carriers had the symptoms of the fever before they discovered the pyramid and it is highly likely that the lord died of the same fever. 2. Two. The entrance hall and a bedroom on the first floor. 3. The fact that he limped just like the thief. 4. He was the grandson of the pyramid's discoverer; he had the largest (untouched) collection of relics from Tut-Enk-Ra's tomb; he had access to the museum. 5. Because he wasn't feeling very well, and perhaps he had something to hide!
Übung 84: 1. Hudson 2. she/Elvira 3. She 4. Hudson 5. Hudson 6. he
Übung 85: 1. bump into 2. moaned 3. went after 4. huge 5. looked 6. middle
Übung 86: "The end justifies the means." Der Zweck heiligt die Mittel.
Übung 87: make out, dropped in, calm down, taken aback, brought along
Übung 88: 1. The mummy was stolen from the museum. 2. Some forensic tests are being conducted. 3. The case will have been solved by Hudson. 4. The tomb was opened straight away. 5. Elvira and Hudson have not been invited by the butler.
Übung 89: 1. Lord Winterbutton raised himself tiredly from his pillows. 2. The thief broke into the house. 3. Before going home, he dropped her off. 4. Hudson is looking forward to his day off. 5. Hudson was always assigned the difficult cases. 6. They broke into the house and stole some portraits. 7. Does he know anything about the mummy theft? 8. The Egyptian culture is really interesting.

Übung 90: 1. quickly 2. kept 3. it must be stored 4. than 5. Without waiting 6. next to the door 7. Luckily
Übung 91: 1. c 2. d 3. b 4. e 5. a 6. i 7. f 8. j 9. h 10. g
Übung 92: 2. Elvira is a friend (who) Hudson can always rely on./Elvira is a friend on whom Hudson can always rely. 3. That's the man (who) the police were looking for. 4. That is the mummy the investigator is looking for. 5. Sir Reginald is the boss Hudson listens to. 6. This is a clue (which) Hudson looked for carefully. 7. That's his friend who is sitting next to him.
Übung 93: 1. label 2. taste 3. size 4. trespassing 5. horizontally 6. torch
Übung 94: 1. upright/horizontal 2. right/wrong 3. forwards/backwards 4. laugh/cry 5. approve/disapprove 6. huge/tiny 7. carefully/carelessly 8. steep/gradual 9. narrow/wide
Übung 95: 1. put 2. held 3. gave 4. swung 5. are 6. said 7. froze 8. had been catapulted 9. could 10. were decorated
Übung 96: 2. will she 3. shall we 4. isn't it 5. does he 6. shouldn't she 7. will you 8. aren't I
Übung 97: 1. I'm going to 2. is going to 3. will 4. I'll 5. you'll 6. I'm not going to 7. I'll 8. are you going to 9. will
Übung 98: 1. on 2. between 3. have 4. width 5. depth 6. alive 7. run away 8. policeman
Übung 99: 2. He must be afraid of dying. 3. He might have hidden them. 4. He must have a deadline to meet. 5. Someone could still be awake. 6. He must have used the access card. 7. Lord Winterbutton might be sleeping.8. They must have been unlucky. 9. He could have used the fire escape.
Übung 100: 1. tricks 2. tomb 3. butler 4. authority 5. caught 6. inspector
Übung 101: "With the disappearance of the mummy!" said Elvira angrily "You mean with the theft of the mummy, just like all the other thefts. Half the relics have been stolen from all around the world." – "I'm afraid you're right, sir. But I had my good reasons." – "And I have good reasons to arrest you, Lord Winterbutton!" said Hudson sternly. – "I'm very sorry, but I can't allow that. It would be my death sentence."
Übung 102: 1. change 2. hurt oneself 3. feel 4. remember 5. enjoy oneself 6. look after oneself
Übung 103: 1. of 2. for 3. for 4. of 5. with 6. about 7. to 8. for 9. to 10. about 11. of 12. at
Übung 104: 1. discussion 2. suspicion 3. advice 4. exclamation 5. enquiry 6. imitation 7. employment
Übung 105: 1. grinned 2. measures 3. asked 4. poison 5. lawyer 6. crime 7. clever 8. trust
Übung 106: 1. shouldn't 2. don't have to 3. couldn't 4. won't 5. was able to 6. mustn't 7. should have obtained

Übung 107: 2. of 3. of 4. in 5. on 6. in 7. in 8. of
Übung 108: 1. I'm ashamed of what I have done. 2. Inspector Hudson took a step forward. 3. The main entrance was surrounded by a large crowd of photographers. 4. He seemed rather excited at the idea of helping Scotland Yard in an investigation. 5. The sports car was driven by either a madman or a reporter. 6. All the equipment had to be transported on camels. 7. When they came to the top of the stairs, they saw a long, dark corridor.
Übung 109: 1. An imitation of Tut-Enk-Ra's tomb. 2. The mummy. 3. Elvira knocked him on the floor. 4. To profit from his family. Every time a Winterbutton died, his family kept a lot of the family's fortune. 5. He intended closing them in the tomb.
Übung 110: 1. gave 2. we'll pull 3. doesn't need 4. will eliminate 5. being 6. heard 7. was overjoyed. 8. you'll celebrate 9. went
Übung 111: 1. Elvira had found a half-open window and carefully pushed it open. 2. His eyes slowly got used to the darkness. 3. He was happy for the insurance agent because her clients would save millions of pounds. 4. Hudson could not believe his eyes because instead of a cellar he had found an Egyptian death chamber. 5. Luckily the butler also seemed to be asleep at this late hour. 6. There was some light on the first floor, so both of them were careful. 7. Despite the late hour it took only a few seconds before a man dressed as a butler opened the door.
Übung 112: 1. of 2. from 3. against 4. for 5. in 6. for
Übung 113: 1. he steals 2. he is stealing 3. he stole 4. he used to steal 5. he was stealing 6. he has stolen 7. he has been stealing 8. he had stolen 9. he had been stealing 10. he is going to steal 11. he will steal 12. he will have stolen 13. he will have been stealing

Lösungen Abschlusstest

Übung 1: 1. is drinking 2. is he doing 3. travels 4. knows 5. is looking 6. is raining
Übung 2: 1. would have enjoyed 2. would like 3. wouldn't put
Übung 3: 1. f 2. c 3. a 4. b 5. d 6. e
Übung 4: 1. January the seventh two thousand and three 2. a quarter to seven 3. tomorrow at noon 4. on the fifth of May 5. ten minutes to six this evening 6. eighteen twelve
Übung 5: 1. at 2. in 3. on 4. in 5. at 6. on 7. in 8. in 9. at
Übung 6: 1. some 2. much 3. any 4. much 5. a lot of 6. a lot of 7. many